Meaningful Movement

A Music Teacher's Guide to Dalcroze Eurhythmics

by Marla Butke, Ph.D. and David Frego, Ph.D.

Jayne Wenner, editor

No part of this publication may be reproduced in any form or by any means, except where indicated as reproducibles, without the prior written permission of the publisher.

Copyright © 2016 by MIE Publications
5228 Mayfield Road
Cleveland, Ohio 44124
(800) 888-7502

www.MusicIsElementary.com

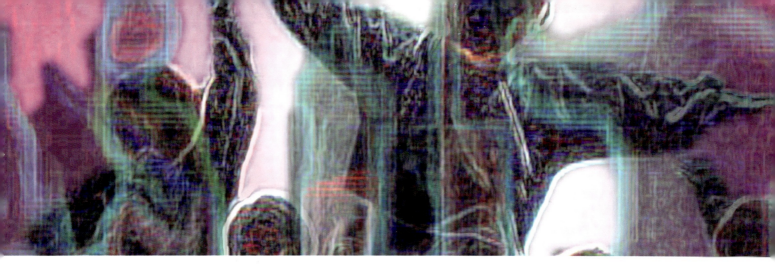

ACKNOWLEDGEMENTS

The authors would like to thank the following people for their contributions to the creation of this book. Without their knowledge and support, this book could not have been written.

Our many Dalcroze teachers and mentors

Our students from whom we have learned so much

Participants in the video recordings

Editor - *Jayne Wenner*

Cover Art - *Shahin Afnan*

Readers - *Nancy Lineburgh, Kristy Piper, Megan Routh, Jerusha Walker*

Colleagues/Contributors - *Fritz Anders, Steven Robbins, Kathy Thomsen*

Photographer/Videographer - *Brandon Fletcher*

Graphic Artist - *Marie Smith, Radiant Graphic Design*

Webmaster - *Aaron Collins*

Endorsements - *Judy Bond, Patricia Sheehan Campbell*

Publishing Consultant - *Roger Sams*

Family - *Jim, Lee, Ryan, Sarah, and Jay*

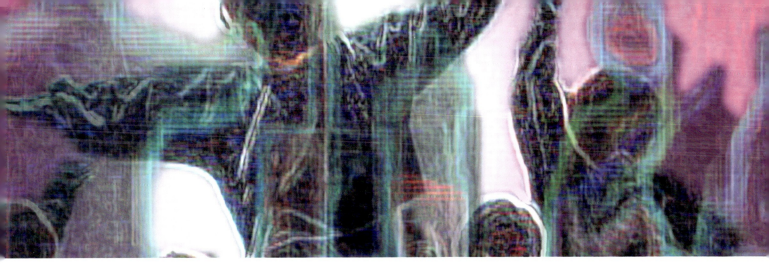

BIOGRAPHIES

Marla Butke, Ph.D., directs the Women's Chorale at Otterbein University, and has taught at Ashland University, Xavier University, and Ohio Wesleyan University. She is a Master Teaching Artist with the American Eurhythmics Society, serves as the vice-president of the board of AES, and is the Ohio Chapter President. Dr. Butke was a contributing author to *Women and Music in America Since 1900*, and has been published in *General Music Today*, *TRIAD*, *Update*, *The Orff Echo*, and *Enrollment Management*. Dr. Butke regularly presents workshops throughout the United States on Dalcroze Eurhythmics. Her most recent article, co-authored by Dr. Frego is entitled, "An Analysis of the Dalcroze Eurhythmics Concept of *Plastique Animée*."

David Frego, Ph.D., is the Blumberg Endowed Professor and Chair of the Department of Music and Dance at the University of Texas at San Antonio, and is President of the American Eurhythmics Society. As an instructor in Dalcroze Eurhythmics, Dr. Frego regularly presents workshops throughout the globe. While performing artists of all ages benefit from rhythmic training, eurhythmics in teacher training is an important focus of Dr. Frego's research. He has published book chapters, DVDs, and articles in both music education journals and medical journals for arts medicine.

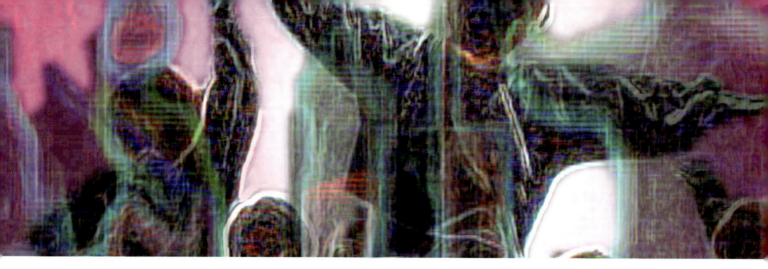

TABLE OF CONTENTS

Title Page **1**
Acknowledgements **2**
Biographies **3**
Table of Contents **4**

Chapter One

Introduction **6**
How to Use this Book **7**
Basic Guidelines **8**
Activities Index of Musical Concepts Taught Through the Dalcroze Approach **9**

Chapter Two

Focus Definition and Purpose **11**
Focus Chart of Activities **11**
Focus Sample Lesson Plan with Assessment **12**
Focus Descriptions of Activities **13**

Chapter Three

Eurhythmics Definition and Purpose **27**
Eurhythmics Chart of Activities **27**
Eurhythmics Sample Lesson Plan with Assessment **29**
Eurhythmics Descriptions of Activities **30**

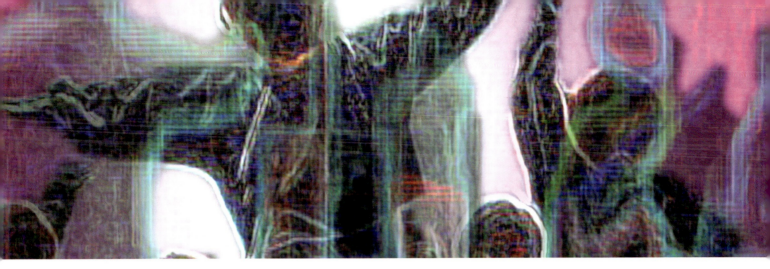

Chapter Four

Expressive Movement/Plastique Animée Short Process/Teacher-Driven Definition and Purpose 79
Expressive Movement/Plastique Animée Short Process/Teacher-Driven Chart of Activities 79
Expressive Movement/Plastique Animée Short Process/Teacher-Driven
　Sample Lesson Plan with Assessment 80
Expressive Movement/Plastique Animée Short Process/Teacher-Driven
　Descriptions of Activities 81
Expressive Movement/Plastique Animée Long Process/Student-Driven Purpose 92
Expressive Movement/Plastique Animée Music Chart with Concepts 92

Chapter Five

Rhythmic Solfège Definition and Purpose 94
Rhythmic Solfège Chart of Activities 94
Rhythmic Solfège Sample Lesson Plan with Assessment 95
Rhythmic Solfège Descriptions of Activities 97

Chapter Six

Piano Improvisation 118
Sequential Lessons 122
Glossary 123
Music Literature List 124
Music Literature List by Genre 126

Meaningful Movement: A Music Teacher's Guide to Dalcroze Eurhythmics

CHAPTER ONE
Introduction to Dalcroze Eurhythmics

"The power of creative imagination permits entry into the future." — Jaques-Dalcroze

Why Eurhythmics? Émile Jaques-Dalcroze developed a philosophy that can strongly impact the future of music education and our society. His concept of Eurhythmics, or good movement, fosters rhythmic integrity and expression using the body as the primary instrument. The philosophy of Dalcroze respects the child and the potential each one holds. Dalcroze stated, "Every child is born an artist; he/she loves to imagine and create." But the philosophy goes beyond the confines of a music curriculum. Implementing Eurhythmics into the curricular structure impacts all students':

- Concentration
- Self-control
- Memory
- Perception of time, space, and energy
- Sense of responsibility
- Social integration
- Coordination and independence of movement
- Sensitivity
- Creativity
- Relaxation

The Preamble to the Mission and Goals of the National Association for Music Education (NAfME) states:

> *Music allows us to celebrate and preserve our cultural heritages, and also to explore the realms of expression, imagination, and creation resulting in new knowledge. Therefore, every individual should be guaranteed the opportunity to learn music and to share in musical experiences.*

The Dalcroze approach is rooted in expression, imagination, and creation, making it an approach that satisfies our music education goals but more importantly, the needs of our children. "It is the job of education to bring out the child's musical nature" (Jaques-Dalcroze).

Meaningful Movement: A Music Teacher's Guide to Dalcroze Eurhythmics

The Dalcroze Eurhythmics approach was developed by musician, dancer, and educator, Émile Jaques-Dalcroze in Switzerland in the early twentieth century. While the approach was initially intended for conservatory students, the application of Eurhythmics soon expanded to the training of musicians, dancers, and actors of all ages. The approach came to the United States mid-century with centers in New York, Pittsburgh, and Cleveland. The American Eurhythmics Society (AES) was formed in 2014 to "continue the work of Dalcroze by providing training opportunities in Eurhythmics for music educators who practice their craft in the classroom or in the private teaching studio. The AES will serve those teachers looking for meaningful ways to include movement rooted in the philosophy of Dalcroze to meet national and state education standards, and to provide authentic assessment opportunities." For more information, visit the website at americaneurhythmics.org.

How to Use This Book

This book contains:

- 206 lessons divided into 4 phases - Introductory/Beginning/Intermediate/Advanced
- 79 pieces of music literature categorized by genre
- Video-link access to view 31 lessons presented by children and adults: **meaningfulmovement-mie.org** / **Access Code - 20161101**
- A cross-referenced index for teaching musical concept
- 4 sequential lessons incorporating key components of the Dalcroze approach
- Sample lesson plans and assessment rubrics
- Piano improvisation ideas
- Brief history of Dalcroze and the approach
- Basic guidelines/principles
- Glossary

The four phases are not meant to represent specific grade levels, rather, they are intended to show sequence based on the students' experience and developmental appropriateness. The four lesson chapters (Focus, Eurhythmics, Expressive Movement/Plastique Animée, Rhythmic Solfège), serve as a collection of teacher-tested sequential activities that teach a variety of music concepts with the goal of educating students in the major tenets of the Dalcroze approach - concentration, rhythmic integrity, artistic movement, and social integration. The book can supplement a variety of music education approaches providing meaningful movement opportunities for students of all ages.

Basic Guidelines/Principles

- **Barefoot is ideal, but often not realistic.** Do not allow flip-flops, heels, noisy shoes, or shoes that restrict safe movement.

- **Incorporate meaningful, expressive movement into each class period.** Dalcroze Eurhythmics can be blended effectively with the other music education approaches.

- **Meaningful movement is different than movement in a game.** It is rhythmic, artistic, responsive, and/or creative.

- **Start where the children are** and build on their current physical, musical, and emotional stages of development.

- **Helping students maintain a steady beat** at the introductory phase of the activities might require the use of a hand drum by the teacher. Building independence without the hand drum is the goal.

- **Social interaction is a key component to this approach.** Engage children often in pairs and small groups.

- **Space is integral to the process but can be creatively organized.** Arrange the classroom for maximum space. If the maximum space is small, have some students do non-locomotor movements while others do locomotor movements and switch tasks.

- **Some activities call for the teacher to improvise on the piano.** If you are not comfortable at the piano, read the chapter on piano improvisation to learn new ideas for improvisation. There are many options to being successful. Pentatonic, atonal, and modal harmonies can be effective as well as traditional I, IV, V7 chord progressions. Improvisations need to be clear, simple, and musical.

- **Activities that are non-locomotor should be done standing.** When standing, the students stimulate increased brain activity.

- **Experience first, label second.**

- **Be encouraging and supportive.** The classroom atmosphere should be joyful!

- **Effective classroom management is imperative.** Be consistent with expectations. It can take some time to develop a culture of movement. Be patient and do not give up!

Activities Index of Musical Concepts
TAUGHT THROUGH THE DALCROZE APPROACH

Rhythm

- Pulse
  32, 24
- Steady beat
  1, 4, 5, 6, 7, 8, 10, 11, 12, 13, 15, 16, 17, 19, 20, 21, 22, 25, 26, 28, 29, 30, 31, 33, 34, 39, 42, 44, 45, 46, 47, 48, 49, 52, 54, 59, 60, 68, 115, 116, 117, 119, 124, 125, 144, 146, 149
- Durations
  36, 42, 43, 47, 52, 56, 57, 58, 64, 65, 68, 69, 73, 74, 82, 83, 84, 85, 95, 98, 99, 103, 112, 124, 125, 173, 182, 186, 194, 197, 199, 205
- Rhythmic patterns
  38, 80, 85, 86, 135, 144, 147, 149, 158, 164, 186
- Macro-beat/micro-beat
  46, 78, 89, 90, 98, 105, 106, 109, 132, 134, 135, 136, 153, 154
- Subdivision
  46, 47, 74, 99, 108, 109, 192
- Tempo
  10, 35, 48
- Ritardando/accelerando
  59, 135, 151
- Simple, compound, mixed, complex meter
  8, 17, 46, 48, 49, 51, 52, 54, 55, 58, 69, 70, 71, 72, 73, 75, 83, 88, 89, 90, 91, 92, 93, 105, 106, 107, 129, 135, 138, 142, 146, 150, 151, 156, 157, 186, 195, 199
- Syncopation
  60, 86, 87, 103, 136, 137, 160, 199
- Complementary rhythms
  55, 78, 79, 110, 111
- Polyrhythms
  100, 101, 102, 156
- Augmentation/diminution
  17, 204
- Anacrusis
  45, 50, 51, 70, 71, 72, 75, 76, 77, 92, 98

Expression

- Articulation - *legato, staccato, marcato*
  36, 118, 119, 120, 121, 123, 124, 125, 127, 128, 130, 132, 141, 142, 143, 145, 146, 148, 150, 151, 152, 156, 157, 158, 161, 162, 163, 164
- Dynamics
  117, 124, 125, 129, 146, 147, 149, 154, 155, 157, 158, 159, 160, 162, 163, 164
- Tension and relaxation
  133, 139, 155
- Consonance/dissonance
  126, 134, 155, 159
- Accent
  18, 19, 99, 154
- Rubato
  129, 142, 151, 160, 161, 163
- Nuance
  75, 129, 145, 150, 152, 155, 156, 157, 158, 159, 160, 161, 162, 163, 164

Melody
- High-low/pitch range recognition
  42, 68, 99, 116, 143, 166, 171, 190, 196
- Steps and skips, contour
  141, 148, 151, 152, 174, 183, 188, 189, 197, 202
- Major/minor scales
  169, 173, 179, 180, 182, 183, 184, 185, 186, 187, 193, 197, 198, 199, 200
- Phrasing
  45, 57, 59, 64, 76, 77, 80, 82, 94, 95, 103, 104, 120, 127, 128, 130, 150, 152, 161, 163
- Melodic rhythm
  39, 62, 63, 64, 65, 76, 95, 107, 110
- Dichords
  174, 189
- Trichords
  188, 202

Harmony
- Chord differentiation/identification
  41, 66, 67, 96, 113
- Cadences
  97, 114
- Major/minor tonality
  41, 66, 96, 113
- Modes
  182, 193, 197, 198, 199

Texture
- Interrupted, overlapping, and continuous canon
  7, 16, 25, 61, 64, 67, 94, 95, 192, 193, 201, 203, 204

Tone Color
- Voices
  147, 149, 157
- Instruments
  142, 148, 163

Form
- Binary
  91
- Ternary
  158
- 12 bar Blues
  67
- Rondo
  86, 154

CHAPTER TWO
FOCUS *Definition & Purpose*

The purpose of a focus activity is to direct a student's attention to a particular task.
Focus activities can help students look for and experience patterns that translate to hearing or performing patterns in music. These activities can also serve the function of awakening muscle groups as preparation for movement experiences. A focus activity assists in clearing the mind and preparing the body with the intention of supporting on-task behaviors in the music classroom. Focus activities encourage the mind to think ahead of real time - a skill necessary for the performing arts.

All of these activities can be perceived as both focus over time and depth of focus in the moment. Repetitive activities increase focus over time. New activities with layers of increasingly difficult challenges enhance the depth of focus.

FOCUS Chart of Activities

INTRODUCTORY	BEGINNING	INTERMEDIATE	ADVANCED
1. Alphabet/Number	8. Alphabet/Number	17. Alphabet/Number	26. Alphabet/Number
2. Name Gestures	9. Name Gestures	18. Name Gestures	27. Name Gestures
3. Yes/No Opposites	10. Start/Stop Inverse with New Tempi	19. Passing the Beat	28. Apple/Pear Opposites
4. Start/Stop and Inverse	11. Passing the Beat	20. Diminishing/Adding the Beat	29. Finger Tap
5. Sequencing the Beat	12. Diminishing/Adding the Beat	21. Apple/Pear Opposites	30. Simultaneous Conducting of Two and Three
6. Passing the Beat	13. Apple/Pear Opposites	22. Backwards Spelling	31. Bizz/Buzz
7. Body Percussion Canon	14. Ear/Nose Switch	23. Finger/Thumb Exchange	
	15. Backwards Spelling	24. Finger Conundrum	
	16. Body Percussion Canon	25. Body Percussion Canon	

Meaningful Movement: A Music Teacher's Guide to Dalcroze Eurhythmics

FOCUS Sample Lesson Plan with Assessment

"DIMINISHING/ADDING THE BEAT"

Beginning Phase

Objectives:

1. The student will clap a steady beat using a circular motion.
2. The student will demonstrate counting patterns from one to six.
3. The student will interact in a large group.

National Standards:

Performing and Responding

Procedure:

1. Students stand in a circle.
2. One student claps six beats using a circular clap and then turns towards the student on the right on beat six and passes the beat to that student.
3. The next student claps six beats and continues the process.
4. When it gets back to the first student, five beats get passed around the circle.
5. Keep reducing the beats to be passed until they are passing just one beat.
6. Students should count inside their heads.
7. Each student claps one beat and then passes the beat to the next student.
8. When it gets back to the first student, then that student passes two beats to the next student.
9. Add a beat each time it gets back to the first student until six beats are being passed.
10. Students should count inside their heads.
11. Encourage the students to create a phrase by having the set of claps move in a direction or shape.

Assessment:

1. The teacher will observe the student clapping a steady beat in a circular motion.
2. The student will demonstrate counting patterns from one to six.
3. The student will verbally reflect upon the success of the experience as being part of a group.

FOCUS: Diminshing/Adding the Beat Rubric

	UNSATISFACTORY	PROGRESSING	SATISFACTORY	OUTSTANDING
Steady Beat	Does not show a steady beat any or most of the time and does not use a circular clap.	Inconsistently shows a steady beat.	Usually shows a steady beat.	Always shows a steady beat and uses a circular clap.
Counting Patterns	Incorrectly performs the indicated number of beats all or most of the time.	Inconsistently performs the indicated number of beats.	Usually performs the indicated number of beats.	Always performs the indicated number of beats.
Social Interaction	Does not turn towards the next person to pass the clapped beat. Shows apathy about performing the activity.	Turns toward the next person when passing the clapped beat with a lack of energy.	Turns toward the next person when passing the clapped beat with inconsistent energy and enthusiasm.	Turns toward the next person when passing the clapped beat with consistent energy and enthusiasm.

FOCUS Description of Activities

Introductory Phase

1. Alphabet/Number

Concepts: Steady beat, patterns

a.
- Students stand in a circle.
- Students point to themselves and say "1."
- Students point to the teacher who says, "A."
- Students point to themselves and say "2."
- Students point to the teacher who says, "B."
- Continue process through to "26," "Z."
- Switch by having the students point to themselves and say the letters and the teacher says the numbers.

b.
- Teacher divides the group in half (red group and green group) and has the students stand facing each other.
- Red group points to themselves and says the letter while the green group points to the red group.
- Red group points to the green group and the green group says the corresponding number.
- Continue through to "Z-26."

c.
- Students stand in a circle.
- Designate one hand for the letters and one hand for the corresponding number.
- Students say the letters/numbers and show steady beat with hands for "A-1" to "E-5" and stop.

WHILE "STANDING" IS INDICATED IN MOST ACTIVITIES, THE TEACHER SHOULD MAKE THE NECESSARY ACCOMODATIONS FOR THOSE STUDENTS WHO ARE PHYSICALLY CHALLENGED.

2. **Name Gestures** (video clip)

   Concepts: Social integration, body awareness

   - Students stand in a circle.
   - Students create a series of gestures that represents their individual names. These gestures can be directly related to the name or a syllable of the name, or could be a gesture that reflects the student's personality.
   - Students perform their gestures individually while saying their names, and the class repeats the gesture and the name.

3. **Yes/No Opposites**

   Concepts: Disassociation, quick reaction

   - Students stand in a circle.
   - Students nod and say "yes" at the same time, followed by shaking their heads and saying "no."
   - Students practice saying the word "yes" but shake their heads "no."
   - Students practice saying the word "no" but nod their heads "yes."
   - Teacher asks yes/no questions and the students respond verbally with their correct response but do the opposite head motions.

- Suggested questions:
  - Do you have a pet?
  - Do you have a brother?
  - Do you have a sister?
  - Do you like pizza?
  - Do you play a sport?
  - Do you like to read?
  - Do you like video games?
  - Have you ever gone camping?
  - Do you know how to ride a bike?
  - Do you like music class?
- Teacher asks yes/no questions and the students respond verbally with the opposite response but do the appropriate head motions.

4. Start/Stop and Inverse (video clip)

Concepts: Steady beat, quick reaction

- Students stand in their self-spaces.
- When the teacher plays the piano, the students walk the beat; and when the teacher stops playing, the students stop walking.
- Inverse - students stand still while the teacher plays a melody for sixteen steady beats on the piano. When the teacher stops, the students walk that tempo in silence.

5. Sequencing the Beat

Concepts: Steady beat, quick reaction, body awareness

- Students stand in their self-spaces.
- Students walk to the steady beat of the teacher playing a hand drum.
- Teacher calls out a number less than ten and the students walk for that many counts, and then the students freeze for the same number of counts.
- Students should count inside their heads.
- Resume walking until the teacher calls out another number.
- Teacher adds another action for that number of beats, i.e. "tap your shoulder."
- Continue the process with some actions to be heard and some to be silent.
- Ask the students to suggest actions.

6. Passing the Beat

Concepts: Steady beat, cooperative learning

- Students stand in a circle.
- Teacher claps four beats and then, going around the circle, each student individually claps one beat maintaining the tempo the teacher has indicated.

7. Body Percussion Canon

Concepts: Steady beat, interrupted and continuous canon, body awareness

- Students stand in their self-spaces.
- Teacher shows the beat using body percussion in four-beat phrases using quarter notes.
- Students echo the body percussion phrase.
- Teacher uses another part of the body to show the four beats and the interrupted canon continues.
- Teacher shows the beat using body percussion in four-beat phrases and as the students echo the pattern, the teacher does another four-beat pattern at the same time (continuous canon).

Beginning Phase

8. Alphabet/Number

Concepts: Steady beat, patterns, inner hearing, quick reaction, triple meter

a. Students stand in a circle.
   - Designate one hand for the letters and one hand for the corresponding number.
   - Students say the letters/numbers and show the steady beat with the hands for the entire alphabet and twenty-six numbers, with the last pair being "Z-26." (video clip)

b. Students stand in a circle.
   - Students speak two pairs out loud, then two internally: "A-1, B-2, - - - -, E-5, F-6, - - - - I-9, J-10, etc." (video clip)

c. • Students stand in a circle.
   - Designate a student leader to stand in the center of the circle.

- When the leader's arm is down, everyone says the combination out loud and uses their hands to keep the beat.
- When the leader's arm goes up, the students continue saying the combination silently in their heads, still showing the beat with their hands.

d.
- Students stand in a circle.
- To indicate triple meter, the letter goes in one hand for beats one and two and the number goes in the other hand for beat three. Students sway to the dotted half note macro-beat.

e.
- Students stand in a circle.
- To indicate triple meter, the letter goes in one hand for beat one, the number goes in the other hand for beat two, and touch an appropriate part of the body for beat three.

9. Name Gestures

Concepts: Social integration, body awareness

- Students stand in a circle.
- Students create a series of gestures that represents their names. These gestures can be directly related to the name or a syllable in the name, or could be something that reflects the student's personality.
- Students perform their gestures individually while saying their names, and the class repeats the gesture and name.
- Students perform their gestures individually without saying the name, and the class repeats the gesture only.

10. Start/Stop Inverse with New Tempi

Concepts: Steady beat, tempo, quick reaction

- Students stand in their self-spaces.
- Teacher improvises sixteen beats on the piano followed by the students walking the steady beat in the tempo the teacher had been playing.
- When the teacher starts improvising, this time in a new tempo, the students stop and follow the same process.

TEACHER CAN USE A HAND DRUM INSTEAD OF IMPROVISING ON THE PIANO. *teacher tip*

11. Passing the Beat

Concepts: Steady beat, cooperative learning

- Students stand in a circle.
- Each student in the circle claps twice; one to accept and one to pass.
- Student "A" claps on one side turning toward a neighbor, then pivots to the neighbor on the other side and sends the clap to that student.
- Student "B" accepts that clap, and then pivots to the neighbor on the other side and sends the clap on to student "C," etc.
- Keep the two claps steady until it comes back to student "A."
- If any student feels the tempo is increasing, that student can bring it back to the original tempo.

12. Diminishing/Adding the Beat

Concepts: Steady beat, patterns

- Students stand in a circle.
- One student claps six beats using a circular clap and then turns towards the student on the right on beat six and passes the beat to that student.
- The next student claps six beats and continues the process.
- When it gets back to the first student, then five beats get passed around the circle.
- Keep reducing the beats to be passed until they are passing just one beat.
- Each student claps one beat and then passes the beat to the next student.
- When it gets back to the first student, then that student passes two beats to the next student.
- Add a beat each time it gets back to the first student until six beats are being passed.
- Encourage the students to create a phrase by having the set of claps move in a direction or shape.

 **STUDENTS SHOULD COUNT INSIDE THEIR HEADS.**

13. Apple/Pear Opposites

Concepts: Steady beat, patterns, disassociation

- Students stand in a circle.
- When the teacher says "apple," the students say "pear." When the teacher says "pear," the students say "apple."
- Teacher says the fruit patterns in four-beat phrases and then the students say the opposite fruit patterns.

Students demonstrate Ear/Nose Switch

14. Ear/Nose Switch

Concepts: Body coordination, crossing center line

- Students stand in a circle.
- Student places left hand on nose and right hand on left ear (circling in front of left hand).
- When teacher says "switch," the student places right hand on nose and left hand on right ear (crosses center line).
- Teacher says "switch" in a steady tempo.
- Teacher increases the tempo.

15. Backwards Spelling

Concepts: Steady beat, spelling, patterns

- Students stand in a circle.
- Teacher says a three-letter word on beat one, rests on beats two, three, and four, and then the students spell the word forward, one letter per beat, then rest for one beat, and spell the word backwards, one letter per beat.
- Teacher increases the tempo.

16. Body Percussion Canon (video clip)

Concepts: Steady beat, interrupted and continuous canon, body awareness

- Students stand in their self-spaces.
- Teacher shows the beat using body percussion in four-beat phrases.
- Students echo the body percussion phrase (interrupted canon).
- Teacher uses another part of the body to show the four beats and the interrupted canon continues.
- Teacher shows the beat using body percussion in four-beat phrases, and as the students echo the pattern, the teacher does another four-beat pattern at the same time (continuous canon).
- Teacher shows the beat using body percussion in two-beat phrases, and as the students echo the pattern, the teacher does another two-beat pattern in continuous canon.

Meaningful Movement: A Music Teacher's Guide to Dalcroze Eurhythmics

Intermediate Phase

17. Alphabet/Number

Concepts: Steady beat, patterns, augmentation/diminution, meter of five, quick reaction

a.
- Students stand in a circle.
- Designate one hand for the letters and one hand for the corresponding numbers.
- Students say the letters/numbers and show the steady beat with hands for the entire alphabet and twenty-six numbers, with the last pair being "Z-26."

b.
- Students say the numbers first, followed by the letters ("1-A, 2-B").

c.
- Students say two pairs with the letters first, followed by two pairs with the numbers first (A-1, B-2, 3-C, 4-D, E-5…).

d.
- Two durations: Students say the first two pairs as half notes, then the next two pairs as quarter notes.
- Continue alternating the durations.

e.
- Meter of five (three plus two): Students say the letter using one hand and sway in that direction on beats one, two, and three. Students then say the number using the other hand while swaying in the other direction for beats four and five.

f.
- Sing "A-1" on *do*, "B-2" on *re*, etc., going from *do* to *sol* ascending and descending, continuously looping the partial scale until reaching "Z-26."

g.
- Sing "A-1" on *re*, "B-2" on *mi*, etc., going from *re* to *la* ascending and descending, continuously looping the partial scale until reaching "Z-26."

h.
- In a meter of four, students say the letter on beat one, and the number on beat two. Then on beats three and four, the first two students in the circle will each name something that is white. Change colors to red, green, black, etc.
Variation - use names of composers, flowers, fruits, states, cartoon characters, etc.

i.
- Students say the letters first followed by the numbers and when the teacher says "switch," they put the numbers first, followed by the letters.

18. Name Gestures

Concepts: Body awareness, social interaction

- Students stand in a circle.
- Students create a series of gestures that represents their names. These gestures can be directly related to the name or a syllable of the name, or could be a gesture that reflects the student's personality.
- Students perform their gestures individually while saying their names, and the class repeats the gesture and the name.

- Students perform their gestures silently, and the class repeats the gesture without saying the name.
- One student performs the personal gesture and shows the gesture of another student. The student whose gesture was just performed shows the personal gesture, and then shows another student's gesture. Go through the process until everyone's gesture has been performed. The last student shows the gesture of anyone.

19. Passing the Beat

Concepts: Steady beat, cooperative learning

- Students stand in a circle.
- Each student in the circle claps twice; one to accept and one to pass.
- Student "A" claps on one side turning toward a neighbor, then pivots to the neighbor on the other side and sends the clap to that student.
- Student "B" accepts that clap, and then pivots to a neighbor and sends the clap on to student "C," etc.
- Keep the two claps steady until it comes back to student "A."
- If any student feels the tempo is increasing, that student can bring it back to the original tempo.
- Teacher says "switch" to send the clap in the other direction.

20. Diminishing/Adding the Beat

Concepts: Steady beat, patterns

a.
- Students stand in a circle.
- One student claps six beats using a circular clap and then turns towards the student on the right on beat six and passes the beat to that student.
- The next student claps six beats and continues the process.
- When it gets back to the first student, then five beats get passed around the circle.
- Keep reducing the beats to be passed until they are passing just one beat.
- Each student claps one beat and then passes the beat to the next student.
- When it gets back to the first student, then that student passes two beats to the next student.
- Add a beat each time it gets back to the first student until six beats are being passed.
- Encourage the students to create a phrase by having the set of claps move in a direction or shape.

b.
- Students stand scattered throughout the classroom. Each student must remember from whom the clap was received and to whom it was passed in the "a" section of the activity.
- The first student claps six beats using a circular clap and then turns towards the student wherever that student is in the room on beat six and passes the beat to that student.
- Continue the process until the students are passing just one beat.
- Reverse the instructions, going from one beat to six beats.

21. Apple/Pear Opposites

Concepts: Steady beat, patterns, disassociation

a.
- Students stand in a circle.
- When the teacher says "apple," the students say "pear." When the teacher says "pear," the students say "apple."
- Teacher says the fruit patterns in four-beat phrases, and then the students say the opposite fruit patterns.
- Teacher says the fruit in eight-beat phrases.

b.
- When the teacher plays quarter notes on the hand drum, the students follow by clapping eighth notes. When the teacher plays eighth notes, the students follow by clapping quarter notes.
- Teacher plays four-beat phrases in quarter and eighth note combinations, and the students clap the opposite rhythms.
- Teacher plays eight-beat phrases in quarter and eighth note combinations and the students clap the opposite rhythms.

22. Backwards Spelling

Concepts: Steady beat, spelling, patterns

- Students stand in a circle.
- Teacher says a five-letter word on beat one, then rests on beats two, three, and four, then the students spell the word forward one letter per beat, then rest for three beats and spell the word backwards one letter per beat.
- Teacher increases the tempo.

23. Finger/Thumb Exchange

Concept: Body coordination

- Students stand in their self-spaces.
- Students hold out two fists in front, with pointer fingers pointing forward in left hands, and the thumbs pointing up in the right hands.

Students demonstrating Finger/Thumb Exchange

Students demonstrating Finger Conundrum

- Switch hands and have the students try it at their own pace. Do not turn the wrists.
- Switch back and forth maintaining a steady beat.

24. Finger Conundrum

Concepts: Body coordination, crossing center line, cooperative learning

- Students form pairs, facing each other. Student "A" puts arms out, crosses arms, faces palms together, interlocks fingers, and then brings the hands under and towards the chest. Student "B" points to one of the fingers of the other student (without touching) and has the student with the interlocked fingers try to lift the finger. Student "B" continues to point to various fingers.
- Students trade responsibilities.

25. Body Percussion Canon

Concepts: Steady beat, interrupted and continuous canon, body awareness

- Students stand in their self-spaces.
- Teacher performs a four-beat pattern using body percussion.
- Students echo the teacher.
- Teacher uses another part of the body to show the four beats and the interrupted canon continues.
- Teacher shows the beat using body percussion in four-beat phrases and as the students echo the pattern, the teacher performs another four-beat pattern at the same time (continuous canon).
- Teacher shows the beat using body percussion in two-beat phrases and as the students echo the pattern the teacher does another two-beat pattern in continuous canon.
- Teacher shows the beat using body percussion in a one-beat phrase and as the students echo the pattern, the teacher does another one-beat pattern in continuous canon.

ALLOW THE STUDENTS TO BE THE LEADERS. *teacher tip*

Advanced Phase

26. Alphabet/Number

Concepts: Steady beat, patterns

a.
- Students stand in a circle.
- Designate one hand for the letters and one hand for the corresponding numbers.
- Students say the letters/numbers and show the steady beat with hands for the entire alphabet and twenty-six numbers with the last pair being "Z-26."

b.
- Students say the first pair as half notes, followed by the next pair as quarter notes.
- Repeat the pattern.

c.
- Three durations: Students say the first two combinations as whole notes, the second pair as half-notes, and the third pair as quarter-notes. Continue the pattern until "Z-26."

d.
- Sing "A-1" on *do*, "B-2" on *re*, etc., going from *do* to *sol* ascending and descending, continuously looping the partial scale until reaching "Z-26."
- Divide the class in half - one group starts on *do* and the other group on *so*.
- Divide the class in thirds - one group starts on *do*, one group starts on *mi* and one group starts on *sol*.

e.
- Sing "A-1" on *re*, "B-2" on *mi*, etc., going from *re* to *la* ascending and descending, continuously looping the partial scale until reaching "Z-26."
- Divide class in half - one group starts on *re* and the other group on *la*.
- Divide class in thirds - one group starts on *re*, one group starts on *fa* and one group starts on *la*.

f.
- Students say the letters going forward and the numbers going backward ("A-26, B-25").

g.
- Students say the letters going backward and the numbers going forward ("Z-1, Y-2").

h.
- In a meter of four, the teacher calls out a letter on beat one followed by three beats of rest. On the following beat one, the students say the corresponding number ("S, rest, rest, rest, 19, rest, rest, rest").

i.
- Students begin with letters first followed by the corresponding numbers going forward. When the teacher says "red" the students say the pairs going backwards. When the teacher says "green" the students say the pair forward again.

27. Name Gestures

Concepts: Body awareness, social interaction

- Students stand in a circle.
- Students create a series of gestures that represents their names. These gestures can be directly related to the name or a syllable or could be something that reflects the student's personality.
- Students individually perform their gestures while saying their names, and the class repeats the gesture and name.
- Students perform their gestures individually without saying the name, and the class repeats the gesture only.
- One student performs the personal gesture and does the gesture of another student. The student whose gesture was just done does the personal gesture and then does another student's gesture. Go through the process until everyone's gesture has been performed. The last student performs the gesture of anyone.
- Teacher plays the beat on the drum and the students do their individual gestures one at a time fitting it into four beats.
- Teacher plays the beat on the drum and the students do their individual gestures fitting them into four beats at a time and then performs each student's gesture going around the circle clockwise as a class canon. All of this is performed simultaneously.

28. Apple/Pear Opposites

Concepts: Steady beat, patterns, disassociation, social interaction

a.
- Students stand in a circle.
- When the teacher says "apple," the students say "pear." When the teacher says "pear," the students say "apple."
- Teacher says the fruit patterns in four-beat phrases, and then the students say the opposite fruit patterns.
- Teacher says the fruit in eight-beat phrases.

b.
- When the teacher plays quarter notes on the hand drum, the students follow by clapping eighth notes. When the teacher plays eighth notes, the students clap quarter notes.
- Teacher plays four-beat phrases in quarter and eighth note combinations, and the students clap the opposite rhythms.
- Teacher plays eight-beat phrases in quarter and eighth note combinations and the students clap the opposite rhythms.
- Students form pairs. Facing each other, they put their left hands out in front of each other with palms up, and place the right hand over the other student's left hand preparing to tap gently with their fingertips the appropriate rhythms. It is important that the vertical space is adjusted appropriately with the note values. Teacher plays a four-beat pattern and student "A" taps the teacher's rhythm and student "B" taps the opposite rhythm simultaneously.

29. Finger Tap (video clip)

Concepts: Steady beat, body coordination

- Students stand in their self-spaces.
- Students warm-up by tapping their thumbs to various other fingers in both hands at the same time (thumb to pointer, then thumb to middle, thumb to ring, thumb to little finger) while maintaining a steady beat.
- Students tap their thumbs to various other fingers in both hands while maintaining a steady beat with the objective being to not tap the same fingers in both hands.

30. Simultaneous Conducting of Two and Three (video clip)

Concepts: Steady beat, patterns, body coordination

- Students stand in a circle.
- Students conduct a two pattern in the left hand and add the three pattern in the right hand (beat stays the same).
- Variations - switch patterns in the hands and change tempi.

 **KEEP THE PATTERN ANGULAR FOR SUCCESS.**

31. Bizz Buzz

Concepts: Steady beat, multiplication, social interaction

- Students stand in a circle.
- Students count off around the circle. When a student gets to the number five (or a multiple of five), it is replaced with "bizz" instead of the number and the counting switches directions. When a student gets to seven, a multiple of seven, or a number with seven in it, it is replaced with "buzz" and then it switches direction.
- When a student gets to thirty-five, it is replaced with "bizz/buzz," and does not change direction.
- The game stops at fifty.
- Start with different people so the students do not start to memorize what number they will have.
- The teacher can play the drum to keep a steady beat as each number is called out.

 **THIS CAN BE PLAYED COMPETITIVELY. THE STUDENTS WHO MAKE A MISTAKE SIT DOWN.**

CHAPTER THREE
EURHYTHMICS *Definition & Purpose*

Eurhythmic activities involve purposeful movement implemented to increase rhythmic integrity and to teach a variety of musical concepts. Although there is emphasis placed on steady beat, the ultimate goal is to experience what is happening between the beats, therefore creating a sense of continuous flow and the unification of time, space, and energy.

Feeling the rhythm internally and showing the rhythm externally are crucial to the growth of a musician.

EURHYTHMICS Chart of Activities

INTRODUCTORY	BEGINNING	INTERMEDIATE	ADVANCED
32. Finding One's Own Personal Pulse	44. Exploring Pulse and Beat	70. Simple Meters with Racquetball	100. Polyrhythms - Two Against Three
33. Steady Beat with Walking and Counting	45. Disappearing Beat	71. Duple and Triple Meter with Rolling Racquetballs	101. Polyrhythms - Five against Two
34. Steady Beat by Passing the Ball	46. Macro-beat/Micro-beat	72. Star Shape with Racquetballs	102. Polyrhythms - Three Against Two - "Après un Rêve"
35. Walking the Beat at Various Tempi	47. Hip and Hop/ Subdivision	73. Walking Ostinato Patterns While Conducting	103. Durations, Melodic Rhythm, and Syncopation - "Ivan Sings"
36. Durations with Balloons	48. Conducting - "Press, Hug, Welcome, Lift"	74. Hip and Hop/ Subdivisions	104. Augmentation/ Diminution
37. Articulations with Balloons	49. Walking the Beat/ Conducting Simple Meters	75. Anacrusis Phrases with Text	105. Meter of Seven - "Mikrokosmos"
38. Walking Various Rhythmic Patterns	50. Anacrusis/Crusis/ Metacrusis Analogies	76. Anacrusic and Crusic Phrases - Name that Tune	106. Meter of Nine - "Blue Rondo à la Turk"
39. Distinguishing Between Beat and Melodic Rhythm	51. Meters with Racquetballs	77. Anacrusic Phrases - "Clowns"	107. Changing the Meter of a Folk Song
40. Walking Melodic Rhythms of Folk Songs	52. Exploring Compound Meter	78. Complementary Beats Reversal	108. Groups of Twelve
41. Harmonic Dictation with I and V7	53. Compound Meter - "Row, Row, Row Your Boat"	79. Complementary Rhythms - "The Happy Farmer"	109. Subdivisions of the Macro-beat
42. Walking Bass/ Clapping Treble	54. Mixed Meter with "Double Trouble"	80. Anapest/Dactylic Phrases	110. Complementary Rhythms - "Scherzo on Tenth Avenue"

Meaningful Movement: A Music Teacher's Guide to Dalcroze Eurhythmics

EURHYTHMICS Chart of Activities, continued

INTRODUCTORY	BEGINNING	INTERMEDIATE	ADVANCED
43. Basic Movements: Walking, Running, Skipping, Gliding, Jumping	55. Meter of Five - Thread Pull	81. Shifting Accents with Racquetballs	111. Complementary Rhythms - "The Happy Farmer"
	56. Durations with Elastics	82. Durations and Melodic Rhythm - "Ivan Sings"	112. Multi-layered Rhythmic Reading
	57. Durations - "Ivan Sings"	83. Measure by Measure Durations	113. Harmonic Dictation with i, iv, V7, VI
	58. Measure by Measure Durations	84. Rhythmic Ostinato - "Symphony #7, 2nd Movement"	114. Cadence Dictation
	59. Accelerando - "In the Hall of the Mountain King"	85. Rhythm Focus - "America"	
	60. Syncopation with "Running"	86. Drumming Improvisation with Syncopation	
	61. Interrupted Canon	87. Syncopation - "Hello"	
	62. Melodic Rhythm - "Li'l Liza Jane"	88. Meter of Five - "Mission Impossible Theme"	
	63. Melodic Rhythm - "Rocky Mountain"	89. Meter of Five - "Take Five"	
	64. Melodic Rhythm and Canon - "Are You Sleeping?"	90. Meter of Seven - "Unsquare Dance"	
	65. Rhythm Focus with Folk Songs	91. Mixed Meter - "All You Need is Love"	
	66. Harmonic Dictation with I, IV, V7	92. Mixed Meter - "In Freezing Winter"	
	67. Twelve-Bar Blues	93. Mixed Meter - "Connla's Well"	
	68. Walking Bass/Clapping Treble	94. Overlapping and Continuous Canon	
	69. Rhythmic Dictation	95. Melodic Rhythm and Canon - "Are You Sleeping?"	
		96. Harmonic Dictation with I, IV, V7, vi	
		97. Cadence Dictation	
		98. Rhythmic Dictation - "Minuet" BMV 115	
		99. Walking Bass/Clapping Treble	

EURHYTHMICS Sample Lesson Plan with Assessment

"HARMONIC DICTATION WITH I AND V7"

Introductory Phase

Objectives:

1. The student will walk a steady beat.
2. The student will show differentiation between the I and V7 harmonies.

National Standards:

Performing and Responding

Procedure:

1. Students stand in their self-spaces.
2. Teacher plays a tonic (I) chord in quarter notes and asks the students to walk forward.
3. Teacher plays a dominant-seventh (V7) chord in quarter notes and asks the students to walk backwards.
4. Teacher alternates between playing phrases of the I chord and the V7 chord. Students respond to what is played by walking forward or backward. Phrases should be of various lengths.
5. Repeat the previous procedure, improvising a melody over the chords.
6. Repeat the previous procedure using a folk song that contains only tonic and dominant chords (example - "London Bridge").

Assessment:

1. The teacher will observe the students walking a steady beat.
2. The teacher will observe the students changing movement direction with the change of harmony.

EURHYTHMICS: Harmonic Dictation with I and V7 Rubric

	UNSATISFACTORY	PROGRESSING	SATISFACTORY	OUTSTANDING
Steady Beat	Does not walk a steady beat any or most of the time.	Inconsistently walks a steady beat.	Usually walks a steady beat.	Always walks a steady beat.
Discriminating Between I and V7	Does not change movement direction with change of harmony.	Inconsistently performs the indicated movement direction.	Usually performs the indicated movement direction.	Always performs the indicated movement direction.
Social Interaction	Walks into other students and/or walks into restricted areas.	Does not look over shoulder and walks into students when moving backwards.	Is aware of personal space and does not collide with other students.	Is aware of personal space and does not collide with other students; moves with purpose and energy.

EURHYTHMICS *Description of Activities*

Introductory Phase

32. Finding One's Own Personal Pulse

Concepts: Steady pulse, focus

- Students stand in their self-spaces.
- Students walk around the room at a natural pace on the cue, "go."
- On the teacher's cue of "stop," students should stop with both feet on the floor.
- Repeat, reinforcing the natural walking pace.
- In place of "stop," ask the students to "stop and tap;" freeze the feet and tap the tempo on their sternums.
- Repeat, still reinforcing the natural walking pace.
- Students tap on their sternums while they are walking.
- Repeat, asking the students to check that their tapping is the same tempo as their walking.
- Teacher asks the students to "stop and tap," and then asks them to lower their hands so they just feel the tempo.

33. Steady Beat with Walking and Counting

Concept: Steady beat

- Students stand in their self-spaces.
- Teacher taps the hand drum at a comfortable walking tempo, and students walk.
- Teacher calls out number "six." Students walk six steps and freeze for six beats, then resume walking. Teacher continues to play the beat on the hand drum throughout.
- Teacher calls out another number between five and ten. Students walk that number of steps, and then freeze for the same number of beats.
- Students click their tongues in place of walking.
- Teacher asks the students to add other actions to move to the phrases; stamp, pat shoulders, jump, move hips, etc.
- Teacher calls out numbers between two and five for more of a challenge.
- Teacher calls out any number between ten and fifteen beats.

34. Steady Beat by Passing the Ball

Concepts: Steady beat, crossing the mid-line

- Students stand in a tight circle with shoulders almost touching, right arms behind them, and left hands extended from the elbows, palms up.
- Teacher stands in the center and places a ball or beanbag in the hand of one student.
- Teacher and students use the words, "pass and pass and pass...".
- On the word pass, the student passes the ball across the mid-line and into the hand of the person on the right. The ball continues to be passed around the circle to a steady beat.
- When the students are ready, add more balls into the circle.
- Change hands to right hand extended and pass to the left.
- Add different shaped items such as erasers, small plush toys, keys, etc.

35. Walking the Beat at Various Tempi

Concept: Moving faster and slower than the personal tempo

- Students stand in their self-spaces.
- Teacher improvises four measures in common time at the piano, preceded by four steady beats so the students know the tempo. After the four-beat introduction, students begin walking to the beat of the given tempo.
- Teacher improvises four-measure phrases at contrasting tempi. Students begin walking to the beat of the given tempo after each four-beat introduction.
- Teacher asks the students to stand still and listen to four measures of an improvisation. When the improvisation ends, the students walk in silence at that tempo. Teacher assists the students in knowing when the four measures end.
- Teacher plays four measures in a new tempo. Students stand still during the music and move during the silence.

36. Durations with Balloons

Concepts: Whole note, half note, quarter note

- Students stand in their self-spaces.
- Students blow up and tie balloons.
- Students tap the balloons keeping them up in the air for the length of whole notes, half notes, and quarter notes as the teacher improvises on those durations at the piano or plays the hand drum.

37. Articulations with Balloons

Concepts: *Staccato* and *legato*

- Students stand in their self-spaces.
- Students blow up and tie balloons.
- Students tap the balloons with the tips of their fingers in a *staccato* manner keeping them up in the air as quarter notes as the teacher improvises on the piano.
- Students keep their hands on the balloons pushing them through space for four beats to show a phrase in a *legato* manner as the teacher improvises on the piano.

 **IF STUDENTS ARE YOUNG, PREPARE THE BALLOONS AHEAD OF TIME.**

38. Walking Various Rhythmic Patterns

Concepts: Internalizing short rhythmic patterns

- Students stand in their self-spaces.
- Teacher plays two measures of quarter notes on the piano, and students respond by walking the rhythm.

- Teacher plays two measures of half notes, and students respond by walking the rhythm.

- Teacher plays a rhythmic pattern of two quarter notes and one half note for two measures, and the students respond by walking the rhythm.

- Teacher plays one half note and two quarter notes for two measures, and the students respond by walking the rhythm.

- Teacher plays quarter note, quarter note, two eighth notes, quarter note for two measures, and the students respond by walking the rhythm.

- Teacher writes the last three patterns on the board, and the students identify them after moving to them.

39. Distinguishing Between Beat and Melodic Rhythm

Concepts: Steady beat, melodic rhythm, quick reaction

- Students stand in their self-spaces.
- Students sing a familiar folk song and walk the beat.
- Students sing the song and walk the melodic rhythm.
- Students sing the song and begin by walking the beat. When the teacher gives a signal on the hand drum, the students walk the melodic rhythm.
- Teacher continues to give signals as the students change back and forth.

40. Walking Melodic Rhythms of Folk Songs

Concepts: Melodic rhythm, rhythmic memory

- Students stand in their self-spaces.
- With a hand drum, the teacher taps the melodic rhythm of the first phrase of a known folk song. Teacher keeps repeating the phrase and asks the students to step the phrase upon repeated hearings.
- Teacher asks the students to identify the song.
- Students walk and sing the phrase.
- Teacher adds more phrases of the song, continuing the same process.

41. Harmonic Dictation with I and V7

Concepts: Major tonality, chord identification

- Students stand in their self-spaces.
- Teacher plays a tonic (I) chord in quarter notes and asks the students to walk forward.
- Teacher plays a dominant-seventh (V7) chord in quarter notes and asks the students to walk backwards.
- Teacher alternates between playing phrases of the I chord and the V7 chord. Students respond to what is played by walking forward or backward. Phrases should be of various lengths.
- Repeat the previous procedure, improvising a melody over the chords.
- Repeat the previous procedure using a folk song that contains only tonic and dominant chords (example - "London Bridge", next page).

London Bridge

Traditional

42. Walking Bass/Clapping Treble

Concepts: Steady beat, pitch range recognition, durations, quick reaction

- Students stand in their self-spaces.

- Teacher plays continuous quarter notes in the low range of the piano, and the students walk the beat. Then the teacher plays continuous quarter notes in the high range of the piano, and the students stop walking and clap the beat. Vary the range every four to twelve measures for a quick reaction exercise.

43. Basic Movements: Walking, Running, Skipping, Gliding, Jumping (video clip)
(See chapter seven for piano music examples.)

Concepts: Follow the music, durations

- Students stand in their self-spaces.

- Teacher plays walking music (four measures of improvisation in common time) at the students' comfortable walking tempo. Students walk through the space.

- Teacher plays running music (double the speed of walking, eight measures in common time) and students respond.

- Teacher plays skipping music (eight measures of 6/8 emphasizing the quarter-eighth relation) and the students respond.

- Teacher plays gliding music (eight measures of 3/8 emphasizing the third eighth note) and the students respond by swaying arms from side to side, and sliding the feet like skaters, to the dotted quarter note beat.
- Teacher plays jumping music (eight measures of 2/4 emphasizing the low note in the piano for beat one and the high notes for beat two). Students bend their knees on beat one and jump in the air on beat two.

STUDENTS WITH LIMITED MOBILITY CAN PAT/TAP THE RHYTHMS WITH A PARTNER.

Beginning Phase

44. Exploring Pulse and Beat

Concepts: Pulse, steady beat

- Students stand in a circle.
- Teacher taps the hand drum at a medium tempo, and the students practice circular clapping to the beat.
- When the teacher says a number, the students rest that many beats but continue to make circles without making a sound.
- Students pass the circular clap around the circle at the predetermined tempo (one clap per student).
- When the teacher says a number, that number of students continues to make circles without making a sound as it goes around the circle.
- When the teacher says "change," the direction of the circle changes.
- Let any student say "change."

45. Disappearing Beat

Concepts: Anacrusis, phrase lengths, steady beat

- Students stand in their self-spaces.
- Teacher plays the beat on the hand drum to establish the tempo. Students walk a phrase of eight beats while counting to eight, changing direction for each phrase.
- Students anticipate the change of direction by applying a movement to the anacrusis on the last beat of the phrase to prepare for the turn in the new direction.
- Students explore different directions and levels.
- Students walk a phrase of eight, then a phrase of seven, taking off one beat at the end of each subsequent phrase until they are down to one beat.

- Students repeat the activity, and the teacher emphasizes the need for an anacrusis on the last beat of the phrases.

- Teacher charts it on the board:

    X X X X X X X X
    X X X X X X X
    X X X X X X
    X X X X X
    X X X X
    X X X
    X X
    X

- Students reverse, starting on beat one, adding a beat to each phrase until students complete an eight-beat phrase.

- Teacher charts it on the board:

    X
    X X
    X X X
    X X X X
    X X X X X
    X X X X X X
    X X X X X X X
    X X X X X X X X

- Combine the two activities, starting with eight beats and decreasing to one. Do not repeat one, but continue back to eight.

- Teacher charts it on the board:

    X X X X X X X X
    X X X X X X X
    X X X X X X
    X X X X X
    X X X X
    X X X
    X X
    X
    X X
    X X X
    X X X X
    X X X X X
    X X X X X X
    X X X X X X X
    X X X X X X X X

Meaningful Movement: A Music Teacher's Guide to Dalcroze Eurhythmics

- Students maintain phrases of eight beats by adding claps to the steps in each phrase so that each phrase has eight beats.
- Students walk eight beats and change direction.
- Students walk seven beats and clap on beat eight. Continue adding one more clap to each phrase.
- Teacher charts it on the board.

        X X X X X X X X
        X X X X X X X O
        X X X X X X O O
        X X X X X O O O
        X X X X O O O O
        X X X O O O O O
        X X O O O O O O
        X O O O O O O O
        O O O O O O O O

- Students start with eight claps, and then start inserting the claps at the ends of the phrases.
- Students clap eight beats while standing in place.
- Students clap seven beats and step on beat eight. Continue.
- Teacher charts it on the board.

        O O O O O O O O
        O O O O O O O X
        O O O O O O X X
        O O O O O X X X
        O O O O X X X X
        O O O X X X X X
        O O X X X X X X
        O X X X X X X X
        X X X X X X X X

- Students start with eight steps and gradually move to eight claps. Following eight claps, insert the steps back in at the end until students are walking eight steps.

Meaningful Movement: A Music Teacher's Guide to Dalcroze Eurhythmics

- Teacher charts it on the board:

  ```
  x x x x x x x x
  x x x x x x x o
  x x x x x x o o
  x x x x x o o o
  x x x x o o o o
  x x x o o o o o
  x x o o o o o o
  x o o o o o o o
  o o o o o o o o
  o o o o o o o x
  o o o o o o x x
  o o o o o x x x
  o o o o x x x x
  o o o x x x x x
  o o x x x x x x
  o x x x x x x x
  x x x x x x x x
  ```

- Add the music, "A Mover La Colita" and repeat the activity.

46. Macro-beat/Micro-beat

Concepts: Steady beat, subdivisions, macro-beat, micro-beat, meter of three, quick reaction

- Students stand in their self-spaces.
- Students walk the beat at a fast tempo as indicated by the teacher playing the hand drum. Teacher should accent beat one in a meter of three.
- Students walk the "slower" beat (dotted half note in the previous tempo) as indicated by the teacher playing the hand drum.
- Teacher plays the dotted half note several times and switches back and forth with the quarter note. Students walk to the indicated rhythms.
- Teacher explains the faster beat as the micro-beat and the slower beat as the macro-beat.
- Teacher plays the music, "Cider House Rules Main Theme" by Portman, and gives cues on the hand drum for walking either the micro-beat or the macro-beat throughout the piece.

47. Hip and Hop/Subdivision (video clip)

Concepts: Steady beat, durations, subdivision, cooperative learning

- Students stand in pairs facing each other.
- Students extend their right hands, palms up, and each student places the left hand over the partner's right hand.
- Teacher taps a steady half note beat on the drum and each student taps gently on the partner's hand, adding vertical space between taps.

- Teacher cues *hip*, and both the teacher and the students tap twice as fast.
- Teacher cues *hop*, and the students return to the original half note tempo.
- Teacher cues *hop*, and the students move to the whole note tempo, extending space upward between taps.
- Repeat these activities, but the teacher will maintain the central tempo of the half note while the students tap twice as fast or twice as slow responding to the teacher's cues.

Students demonstrate the concept Hip and Hop/Subdivision.

- Students stand in a circle and clap with two fingers in a circular motion at a comfortable half note tempo.
- On the teacher's cue of *hip*, the students clap twice as fast (quarter note) and the circular motion becomes smaller.
- On the teacher's cue of *hop*, the students return to the original tempo.
- Repeat the activity to reinforce *hip* and *hop*.
- On the teacher's cue of *hop*, the students clap twice as slow (whole note), making the circular motion twice as large.
- Responding to the teacher's cues of *hip* and *hop*, the students clap twice as fast or twice as slow.
- Repeat the previous steps with walking to the beat and the subdivisions indicated by the teacher.
- Add the recording "Trumpet Concerto in D (Allegro)" by Torelli and the students respond to the teacher's cues of *hip* and *hop* by stepping the beat and the subdivisions.

48. Conducting - "Press, Hug, Welcome, Lift" (video clip)

Concepts: Steady beat, slow and fast tempi, meter of four

- Students stand in their self-spaces.
- Teacher demonstrates the following adapted conducting pattern of four using both arms:
  - **Beat one** - begin with arms straight out, palms down, and press down (say "press")
  - **Beat two** - arms cross body and hug shoulders (say "hug")
  - **Beat three** - arms stretch out horizontally to the sides of the body, palms facing up, (say "welcome")
  - **Beat four** - arms stretch up toward the center of the body, palms facing up, (say "lift")
- Students walk through space, conduct, and say the words at the tempo indicated by the teacher playing the hand drum.
- Students continue the activity as the teacher changes the tempo.
- Students conduct with the music, "Air on the G String" by Bach (slow tempo).
- Students conduct with the music, "Love Song" by Bareilles (fast tempo).

Meaningful Movement: A Music Teacher's Guide to Dalcroze Eurhythmics

49. Walking the Beat/Conducting Simple Meters

Concepts: Steady beat, meters of two, three, four

- Students stand in their self-spaces.
- Teacher demonstrates a traditional two pattern with one hand and the students conduct in two.
- Teacher indicates a tempo on the hand drum and the students walk and conduct a two pattern.
- Teacher changes tempo, and the students walk and conduct a two pattern.
- Students walk and conduct to "Stars and Stripes Forever" by Sousa.
- Teacher demonstrates a traditional three pattern with one hand and the students conduct in three.
- Teacher indicates a tempo on the hand drum, and the students walk the beat and conduct a three pattern.
- Teacher changes tempo, and the students walk and conduct a three pattern.
- Students walk and conduct to Menuet from *Water Music* by Handel.
- Teacher demonstrates a traditional four pattern with one hand and the students conduct in four.
- Teacher indicates a tempo on the hand drum, and the students walk the beat and conduct a four pattern.
- Teacher changes tempo, and the students walk the beat and conduct a four pattern.
- Students walk the beat and conduct to "Tell My Ma" by the Rankin Family.

50. Anacrusis/Crusis/Metacrusis Analogies

Concepts: Anacrusis, crusis, and metacrusis

- Students stand in their self-spaces.
- Students walk through space at their own pace and occasionally stop in front of another student and try to clap once at the same time.
- Students will discuss their success with clapping simultaneously with different partners. Teacher points out the importance of breathing, eye contact, and making a circular clap which involves an arm preparation.
- Teacher explains that breathing, eye contact, and arm preparation are part of the anacrusis; the crusis is the point of contact of the clap; and the metacrusis is the follow through, all shown by the circular clap.
- Teacher asks the students to pretend to sneeze and then discuss which parts were the anacrusis, crusis and metacrusis.
- Teacher asks one student to be the pitcher, one student to be the batter, and one student to be the outfielder. In this baseball analogy, the rest of the class has to clap when the pitcher initiates the throw, when the batter hits the ball, and when the outfielder catches the ball.
- Students discuss the anacrusis, crusis, and metacrusis of each motion.

51. Meters with Racquetballs

Concepts: Duple, triple, quadruple meters; anacrusis, crusis, and metacrusis; time, space, and energy

Student demonstrates Meters with Raquetaballs.

- Students stand in their self-spaces.
- Each student has a racquetball. Have the students experiment with energy and rebound by bouncing them.
- Teacher plays a steady beat on the hand drum, accenting every other stroke to indicate duple meter. The students bounce and catch on the beat and say "bounce, catch."
- Teacher helps the students identify the anacrusis, crusis, and metacrusis of bouncing and catching the ball.
- Teacher changes to a faster tempo of duple meter, and the students bounce and catch the balls.
- Teacher explains that space and energy need to change in order to accurately bounce the ball on the beat at a faster tempo. The concept of time (the tempo), space, and energy is an important part of movement.
- Teacher changes to a slower tempo of duple meter, and the students bounce and catch the ball. Students discuss how they needed to change space and energy to bounce the ball to a slower tempo.
- Teacher changes to triple meter. The students must show a long, melded metacrusis/anacrusis for beats two and three.
- Teacher changes tempo in triple meter. Students respond accordingly, adjusting space and energy to bounce the balls in each tempo.
- Students are sitting on the floor in pairs across from each other. In $\frac{4}{4}$ meter, one student rolls the ball to the other, releasing on beat one, and the other student catches the ball on beat four. That student sends it back on beat one. Teacher indicates the tempo on the hand drum.
- Teacher changes the tempo, and students must adjust space and energy.
- Add recordings to any of the activities.

RACQUETBALLS FIT SMALLER HANDS AND CAN EASILY BE WASHED.

52. Exploring Compound Meter

Concepts: Steady beat, compound meter, quick reaction

- Students stand in their self-spaces.
- Teacher plays repeated dotted quarter notes in $\frac{6}{8}$ meter on the hand drum, or improvises on the piano, and students say, "step" as they step to the beat.

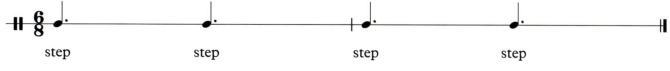

- Teacher plays repeated sets of three eighth notes on the hand drum, or improvises on the piano, and students say, "run-ning and", as they move to that pattern.

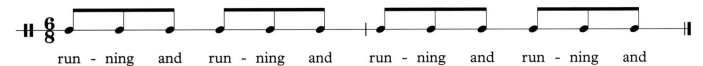

- Teacher alternates between two dotted quarter notes and two sets of three eighth notes and the students say and move to the pattern.

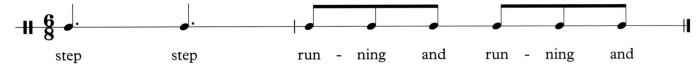

- Teacher plays repeated quarter note/eighth note combinations, and the students say, "skip and," as they move to that pattern.

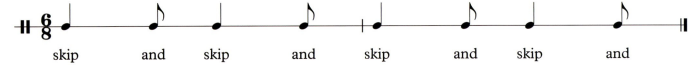

- Teacher plays any of the three patterns on the hand drum, or improvises on the piano, and the students move accordingly.

53. Compound Meter - "Row, Row, Row Your Boat" (video clip)

Concepts: Steady beat, compound meter, durations, quick reaction

- Students sit on the floor in a circle.
- Students clap dotted quarter notes and say, "step" (see activity #52). Teacher plays the rhythm on the hand drum to support the movement.
- Students tap three eighth notes on the floor while saying, "run-ning and" (see activity #52). Teacher plays the rhythm on the hand drum to support the movement.
- Students pat the quarter/eighth pattern on alternating legs, and say, "skip and" (see activity #52). Teacher plays the rhythm on the hand drum to support the movement.
- Teacher randomly plays the three different rhythm patterns on the hand drum, and the students speak the words and do the appropriate body percussion.
- Students pass the hand drum around the circle, and individually play the rhythms that the teacher dictates, while the rest of the class says the rhythm words and performs the body percussion.
- Pass the hand drum around the circle until everyone has had a turn.
- Students stand in their self-spaces.

- Teacher plays the various rhythms on the drum, piano, or barred instrument, and the students move through space to that rhythm while they say the words.
- Repeat the previous step without the students saying the words.
- Students sit in a circle and sing "Row, Row, Row Your Boat" (teach by rote if necessary).

- Teacher performs the body percussion learned in the previous activities while students sing the song again. Have the students rest for a dotted quarter note after "stream" and "dream."
- Students perform the body percussion and sing the song.
- Students perform the body percussion and sing the song with the movement words.
- Using inner hearing, the students perform the body percussion only.
- Students stand in their self-spaces.
- Students sing and perform the locomotor movement learned in the previous activities to show the rhythm of the song. (with optional piano accompaniment).
- Students use inner hearing and perform the locomotor movement (with piano accompaniment).
- Students use inner hearing and perform the locomotor movement (without piano accompaniment).

54. Mixed Meter with "Double Trouble"

Concepts: Steady beat, meters of four, five, seven

- Students stand in their self-spaces.
- Students walk a phrase of four in one direction, clap on beat one, and then repeat several times with each phrase changing direction. Then students walk in phrases of five, changing direction each time. Repeat the process with phrases of seven. Students may count out loud. Teacher is playing the hand drum.
- Students walk in phrases as indicated by the teacher using verbal cues, as the first part of the recorded music is played (introduction - two measures of four, then five measures of four, three measures of five, one measure of seven).

- Students form pairs and tap the meters of four and five into their partners' palms, showing the space through the vertical length.
- Using "Double Trouble" by Williams, students walk the first half of piece. During the eight beats of interlude, they find a partner and perform the tapping in each other's hands until the end of the piece (five measures of four, four measures of five, followed by measures of four until the end of the music).
- Variation with elastics - with the music, students use elastics in pairs to stretch through each of the measures throughout the piece. To form two parallel lines with the elastics, each student has an elastic and holds one end of the elastic wrapped around the wrist and holds the end of the partner's elastic wrapped around the other wrist.
- Variation with racquetballs - with the music, students roll a racquetball to a partner while seated across from each other, for each of the measures; rolling the ball on beat one and stopping the ball on the last beat of the measure, and adjusting space and energy for the changing meters.

WHEN HAVING STUDENTS FORM PARALLEL LINES WITH THE ELASTICS, USE THE VISUAL ANALOGY OF A RIVER.

55. Meter of Five - Thread Pull (video clip)

Concepts: Meter of five, steady beat, complementary rhythms, cooperative learning

- Students stand in pairs facing each other.
- Student "A" pulls an imaginary string off of student "B" for five beats, followed by student "B" pulling an imaginary string off of student "A" for three beats, followed by student "A" pulling for two beats while teacher plays beat on hand drum. Continue the pattern of five/three/two with student "B" pulling the string for five beats, etc.
- Students individually walk five beats in one direction, then three beats in another direction, then two beats in another direction while teacher plays the beat on the hand drum.
- Students clap on beat one, and walk on the complementary beats of the five/three/two pattern.
- Students pull thread from themselves in the five/three/two pattern.

56. Durations with Elastics

Concepts: Half note, quarter note, cooperative learning

- Students stand in pairs facing each other. To form two parallel lines with the elastics, each student has an elastic and holds one end of the elastic wrapped around the wrist and holds the end of the partner's elastic wrapped around the other wrist.
- Teacher plays half notes and quarter notes on the hand drum and the students pull the elastics according to the indicated note value.
- Add "Fight Song" by Platten, and repeat the activity as the teacher cues half notes on the verse and quarter notes on the chorus.

57. Durations - "Ivan Sings"

Concepts: Whole note, half note, quarter note, phrasing, cooperative learning

- Students stand in their self-spaces.
- Teacher plays the first half of "Ivan Sings" by Khachaturian, and the students walk the beat.
- Teacher plays the first half again, and the students walk the half note.
- Teacher plays the first half again, and the students walk the whole note.
- Students get into pairs facing each other with one student being "A" and the other student "B."
- Students put their left arms out with palms up, and place the right hand finger tips on the palm of the partner's left hand.
- Teacher plays the piece and the students tap quarter, half, or whole notes as the teacher indicates with verbal cues.
- The "A" student taps quarter notes and the "B" student taps half notes while the teacher plays the first half of the piece.
- Repeat the last step with the students tapping different durations previously used, changing at the end of each phrase as indicated by the teacher.

58. Measure by Measure Durations

Concepts: Quarter note, eighth note, quarter rest, 4/4 meter, rhythmic improvisation

- Students stand in their self-spaces.
- Students walk four measures of various durations. Teach each measure separately, then put them together.

- Students get into small groups and create a new four-measure pattern.
- Students hold shoulders side by side and move to their compositions as the teacher plays the beat on the hand drum.

59. Accelerando - "In the Hall of the Mountain King" (video clip)

Concepts: Steady beat, phrasing, accelerando

- Students stand in their self-spaces.
- Students walk to the beat as the teacher plays the beat on the hand drum and walk faster as the teacher increases the tempo.
- Students walk fifteen beats in one direction, and on beat sixteen, they stop and make a "boo" face with their hands and whisper, "boo."
- Repeat the last step using the music, "In the Hall of the Mountain King" by Grieg. Students adjust their walking speed to the accelerando in the music.

> **teacher tip** — **REMIND THE STUDENTS TO MAKE THEIR FEET MATCH THE BEAT.**

60. Syncopation with "Running"

Concepts: Steady beat, syncopation

- Students stand in their self-spaces.
- Teacher plays quarter notes on the hand drum or improvises a melody on the piano, and the students walk the beat.
- Teacher plays eighth notes, and the students move to the eighth notes while saying "run-ning."
- Teacher plays eighth notes, and the students say "run-ning" while clapping on the first eighth note and stepping on the second eighth note.
- Repeat last step without clapping on the first eighth note.
- Teacher plays eighth notes, and the students move to the eighth notes while saying, "one and two and three and four and."
- Teacher plays eighth notes on the hand drum, and the students clap on the beat and step on the "and."
- Teacher calls out the "and" of a number (example - "the and of four") and the students clap on all four numbers and step only on the "and" of the number called.
- Repeat last step with different combinations and use multiple "ands."

61. Interrupted Canon (video clip)

Concept: Interrupted canon

- Distribute one necktie to each pair of students.
- Each pair of students faces each other and holds the ends of the tie in the left hands.
- Teacher plays a four-beat phrase on the piano, and in the following four beats of silence, student "A" shows the melodic rhythm, by tapping and sliding the right index finger from left to right along the length of the tie.
- Teacher plays a second four-beat melody, and student "B" shows the melodic rhythm, tapping and sliding the right index finger from left to right along the length of the tie during the following four beats of silence.
- Teacher gradually increases the complexity of the melody to include triplets, sixteenth notes, and syncopation.
- On their own and without the tie, the students listen to the teacher improvise a four-beat melody and then echo-step the melody during the four beats of silence.

Meaningful Movement: A Music Teacher's Guide to Dalcroze Eurhythmics

62. Melodic Rhythm - "Li'l Liza Jane"

Li'l 'Liza Jane

Traditional

Come my love and go with me, Li'l 'Li - za Jane.

Come my love and go with me, Li'l 'Li - za Jane.

O, E - li - za! Li'l 'Li - za Jane.

O, E - li - za! Li'l 'Li - za Jane.

Concepts: Melodic rhythm, inner hearing

- Students stand in their self-spaces.
- Students sing the song.
- Students sing the song while clapping the beat.
- Students sing the song while clapping the melodic rhythm.
- With partners, the students sing the song while tapping the beat with their right hands on the left hands (palms up) of their partners.
- With partners, the students sing the song while tapping the melodic rhythm into their partners' hands.
- With partners, the students sing the song, while one student taps the beat and the other student taps the rhythm.
- Switch roles, and repeat the activity.
- Continue with the students singing the song and one student is tapping the beat and the other student is tapping the rhythm, but at the signal from the hand drum, switch roles.
- Repeat, but at the signal from the hand drum signal, stop singing out loud. At the next signal, resume singing out loud.
- Sing the song and walk the melodic rhythm.
- At the signal from the hand drum, sing internally but continue walking the melodic rhythm. At the next signal, resume singing out loud.

63. Melodic Rhythm - "Rocky Mountain" (video clip)

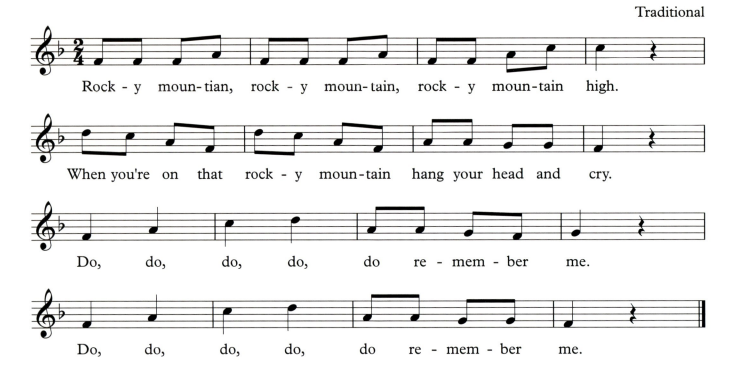

Concepts: Melodic rhythm, melodic recognition

- Students stand in their self-spaces.
- Students sing the song.
- Students sing the song and clap the melodic rhythm.
- Students sing the song and walk the melodic rhythm.
- Teacher walks a phrase of the melodic rhythm, and the students walk it and sing it back (there are duplications in the melodic rhythm so the students have a choice).

64. Melodic Rhythm and Canon - "Are You Sleeping?"

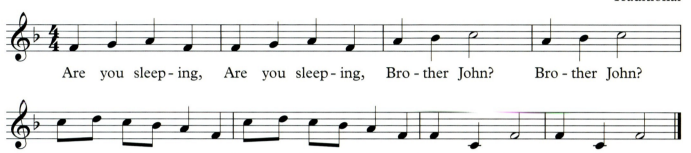

Concepts: Phrasing, melodic rhythm, interrupted and continuous canon, durations

- Students stand in their self-spaces.
- Students sing the song.
- Students sing the song and walk the beat.
- Students sing the song and clap the melodic rhythm.
- Students sing the song, clap the melodic rhythm, and walk the steady beat.
- Students sing the song while the teacher claps the melodic rhythm in canon (eight beats behind).
- Students sing the song and clap the melodic rhythm in canon.
- Students sing the song and walk the melodic rhythm.
- Students sing the song and walk the melodic rhythm in canon.

65. Rhythm Focus with Folk Songs

Concepts: Durations, melodic rhythm

- Students stand in their self-spaces.
- Students sing a familiar folk song that contains quarter notes (example - "Hey, Betty Martin", next page.)

Meaningful Movement: A Music Teacher's Guide to Dalcroze Eurhythmics

Hey, Betty Martin

Traditional

- Students sing the song while clapping the melodic rhythm.
- Students sing the song and only clap on the quarter notes that occur in the song.
- Students sing the song and only walk on the quarter notes.
- Repeat with different songs.
- Repeat with different note values.

66. Harmonic Dictation with I - IV - V7

Concepts: Major tonality, chord identification

- Students stand in their self-spaces.
- Teacher repeatedly plays a tonic (I) chord as quarter notes with the root in the bass. The students walk forward.
- Teacher repeatedly plays a dominant-seventh (V7) chord as quarter notes with the root in the bass. The students walk backwards.
- Teacher repeatedly plays a subdominant (IV) chord as quarter notes with the root in the bass. The students walk sideways.
- Teacher plays a combination of I, IV, and V7 chords and the students walk in the corresponding direction.
- Teacher improvises a melody over the three-chord harmony, and the students walk in the corresponding direction.

TEACHER CAN PLAY VARIOUS INVERSIONS IN THE RIGHT HAND BUT ALWAYS KEEP THE ROOT IN THE BASS.

67. Twelve-Bar Blues

Concepts: Major tonality, chord identification, form

- Students stand in their self-spaces.
- Teacher plays a combination of I, IV, and V7 chords, and the students walk forward for I, backwards for V7, and sideways for IV.
- Teacher plays the twelve bar blues pattern (I, IV, I, I, IV, IV, I, I, V7, IV, I, I), and the students walk in the directions which correspond to the harmonic sequence.
- Teacher plays, "Sad, Sad Day" by Waters, and the students walk in the directions that correspond to the harmonic sequence.

68. Walking Bass/Clapping Treble

Concepts: Steady beat, pitch range recognition, durations, quick reaction

- Students stand in their self-spaces.
- Teacher plays a melody of continuous quarter notes, eighth notes, half notes, or whole notes in the lower range of the piano, changing duration values every eight measures. The students show that note value in their feet, walking around the room.
- Teacher adds a melody of continuous durations in the upper range of the piano, but uses a different note value - either a note value twice as fast or twice as slow as the bass rhythm. Students clap this note value. Teacher can switch the note values played in either hand, including the use of rests. Students simultaneously walk and clap the played note values.

- Keep the ratio 2:1 or 1:2.

69. Rhythmic Dictation

Concepts: Durations, simple meters, literacy

- Students stand in their self-spaces.
- Teacher plays a $\frac{4}{4}$ measure of rhythm on the hand drum and students walk the rhythm.
- Repeat using different rhythms.
- Students read a $\frac{4}{4}$ measure of rhythm from the board and walk the rhythm.
- Repeat using different rhythms.
- Repeat both activities in different meters.

Intermediate Phase

70. Simple Meters with Racquetballs

Concepts: Anacrusis, crusis, and metacrusis; simple meters of two, three, four

a. Introduction

- Students stand in their self-spaces.
- Distribute racquetballs and have students experiment with energy and rebound.
- Teacher plays block chords at the piano, and the students bounce the balls with the beat of the chords.
- Teacher plays at a faster tempo, and the students apply lighter energy to the bounce.
- Teacher plays at a slower tempo, and the students apply stronger energy to the bounce.
- Teacher gradually increases or decreases tempo and the students adjust the amount of energy used to bounce the ball.

b. Meter of two

- Teacher plays in a meter of two. Standing in place, the students bounce on one and catch on two. Remind them to alternate hands.
- Teacher cues to add a step on beat one while continuing the bounce pattern.

c. Meter of three

- Students bounce on beat one, catch on beat two, and make up a movement on beat three.
- Teacher cues the students to add a step on beat one while continuing the bounce pattern.

d. Meter of four

- Students bounce on beat one, catch on beat two, and make up movement gestures for beats three and four.
- Teacher cues to step on beat one while continuing the bounce pattern.

71. Duple and Triple Meters with Rolling Racquetballs

Concepts: Time, space, and energy; anacrusis, crusis, and metacrusis; simple and mixed meters

- Two students sit facing each other approximately six feet apart and share one racquetball.
- Teacher taps a hand drum in a meter of three and students roll the ball to each other.
  - ➢ **Anacrusis** is the preparation to roll.
  - ➢ **Crusis** is the touching of the ball to the floor.
  - ➢ **Metacrusis** is the rolling of the ball across the floor.
- Keeping the same tempo, the teacher taps the hand drum in a meter of two. Students either roll faster or move closer to each other (or a combination).
- Keeping the same tempo, the teacher taps the hand drum in a meter of four. Students either roll slower or move further away from each other (or a combination).
- Students decide what meter is being played and to roll the ball with the appropriate space and energy. The choices are meters of two, three, or four.
- Quick reaction - teacher changes the meter and measures how quickly the students make the change.
- Teacher introduces a meter of five. Students determine the meter and roll the ball with appropriate space and energy.
- Mixed meter: Teacher introduces a meter of seven (3+2+2).
- With three numbers and two students, the leader alternates for each new measure.

> **A METACRUSIS TURNS INTO AN ANACRUSIS WHEN THE STUDENT PICKS UP THE BALL ON THE LAST BEAT OF THE MEASURE AND PREPARES TO BOUNCE THE BALL.**

72. Star Shape with Racquetballs (video clip)

Concepts: Time, space, and energy; meters of two and four; anacrusis, crusis, metacrusis; cooperative learning

a. Meter of two

- Students stand six feet apart from a partner.
- Appoint a few children who are spaced around the room to be ball runners.
- Give one ball to each pair of students.
- Teacher taps a four-beat pattern on the drum and the students bounce the ball on beat one to their partners.
- Partners catch the ball on beat two and move the ball through space in preparation for bouncing on the next beat one.

Meaningful Movement: A Music Teacher's Guide to Dalcroze Eurhythmics

- Practice the anacrusis, anticipating when the ball should land on beat one.
- Keep the ball in motion.

b. Meter of four
- Students are in circles of five.
- Students in the circles count off from one to five.
- Student number one will bounce the ball to student number four, student number four bounces the ball to student number two, two to five, five to three, three to one. This is done in a meter of four with the ball bouncing in the middle of the circle on beat one, caught on beat two with the metacrusis on beats three and four. The teacher plays the hand drum. If the ball is dropped, a ball runner retrieves the ball and hands it back to student number one.
- Student number one should have five balls to start and gradually adds one ball in at a time. The object is to get all five balls going at the same time.
- Add the music, "Ever, Ever, After" by Menken/Schwartz.

73. Walking Ostinato Patterns While Conducting

Concepts: Durations, meter of four, tempo

- Students stand in their self-spaces.
- Students conduct a four pattern.
- Students walk the beat as they conduct a four pattern.
- Students walk two quarter notes/four eighth notes as they conduct a four pattern.

- Repeat with different patterns.
- Repeat at different tempi.
- Repeat in different meters, changing the conducting patterns to fit the new meters.
- Add the teacher improvising at the piano or a recording.

74. Hip and Hop/Subdivisions

Concepts: Time, space, and energy; subdivision, durations

a.
- Students stand in a circle and clap with two fingers in a circular motion in half notes at an adagio tempo.
- On the teacher's cue of *hip*, the students clap twice as fast (quarter note) and circle becomes smaller.
- On the teacher's cue of *hop*, the students return to their original tempo.
- Repeat to reinforce twice as fast and twice as slow.

- On the teacher's cue of *hop*, students clap twice as slow (whole note), making the circular motion twice as large.
- With the teacher's cues of *hip* and *hop*, the students clap twice as fast or twice as slow.
- When the students are clapping the whole note, teacher cues *hip-hip*, which moves the students to the quarter note.

b.
- Facing a partner, the students extend their right hands, palms up, and left hands over their partners' right hands.
- Teacher taps a steady half note on the drum, and the students tap gently on their partners' hands, adding vertical space between taps.
- Teacher cues *hip*, and both the teacher and the students tap twice as fast.
- Teacher cues *hop*, and the students return to their original half note tempo.
- Teacher cues *hop*, and the students move to the whole note tempo, extending space upwards between taps.
- Repeat these activities, but the teacher maintains the central tempo of the half note on the hand drum while the students change to twice as fast and twice as slow.

c.
- Student partners identify themselves as student "A" and student "B."
- Teacher and the students start tapping the central half note tempo.
- Teacher maintains the half note on the hand drum, but calls for student "A" to *hip*, creating a two-to-one ratio.
- Teacher calls for student "A" to *hop*, and both students tap the half note tempo.
- Teacher repeats the same cues for student "B."
- Teacher calls for student "A" to *hip* (quarter note).
- Teacher calls for student "B" to *hop* (whole note) creating a four-to-one ratio.
- Teacher calls for "A" and "B" to switch tasks on cue.

d.
- Teacher taps the central (half note) tempo, and the students walk that tempo on their own.
- Teacher maintains the half note, but calls *hip* and the students walk twice as fast.
- Teacher calls *hop*, and the students return to the half note tempo.
- Teacher calls *hop*, and the students step twice as slow (whole note).
- Teacher returns to *hip* (half note), and asks the students to tap the same tempo while continuing to walk.
- Teacher cues hands to *hip* indicating the hands tap at quarter notes and the feet step to half notes.
- Manipulate the *hip* and *hop* of the hands and feet until feet are stepping the whole note and the hands are tapping the quarter note.

Meaningful Movement: A Music Teacher's Guide to Dalcroze Eurhythmics

- Teacher cues "switch" and hands and feet switch subdivisions.
- Repeat this activity with the teacher at the piano; the hands follow what is played in the higher register, and the feet follow what is played in the lower register. Students respond to the piano without verbal cues.

e.
- Add music "Central Time" by LaFarge
- Teacher plays the music and asks the students to walk the main tempo.
- Teacher cues *hip* or *hop*, and the students walk twice as fast or twice as slow.
- Teacher asks the students to add hand taps in the main tempo. Then the teacher cues *hip* and *hop* at various times for hands and feet.
- Teacher gives the students free choice to step and tap different subdivisions.

75. Anacrusic Phrases with Text

Concepts: Anacrusic and crusic phrases, meters, nuance

- Students stand in their self-spaces.
- Display ten lines from well-known plays on the board.
- Students choose a line and say it repeatedly while walking around the room.
- Teacher asks the students to determine if their line is in duple or triple meter.
  - Example: *Have you gone out of your mind?* (Chekov) triple meter
  - Example: *Blue roses! Oh my gosh, yes—Blue roses!* (Williams) duple meter
- Students choose a new line and walk around the room, determining if the phrase begins with an anacrusis or crusis.
  - Example: *That sounds alarmingly like a compliment.* (Sherwood) anacrusic
  - Example: *We don't know what you want, but we don't want you around here.* (Sheperd) crusic
- Distribute racquetballs and ask the students to choose the accented word in the line and bounce the ball on the accented word while saying the line.
  - Example: *I don't know why I can't keep it. He ain't nobody's mouse.* (Steinbeck) The student may choose to bounce on the word "why" or on the first syllable of "nobody."
- Allow the students to perform their lines individually and have other students determine if the line is anacrusic or crusic; duple or triple; and if the accent is in the right place.

76. Anacrusic and Crusic Phrases: Name that Tune

Concepts: Anacrusic and crusic phrases, melodic rhythm, visually decoding movement

- Students stand in groups of three. Each group thinks of a well-known song and crosses the floor, stepping the melodic rhythm, while using inner hearing of the melody (example - "Happy Birthday").

Meaningful Movement: A Music Teacher's Guide to Dalcroze Eurhythmics

- The other students observe the stepping and determine the name of the song and whether the song is anacrusic or crusic.

THE CHOICES OF SONGS COULD BE SEASONAL, PATRIOTIC, OR SONGS RECENTLY LEARNED IN CLASS.

77. Anacrusic Phrases - "Clowns"

Concepts: Anacrusic and crusic phrases

- Students stand in their self-spaces.
- Teacher reviews definitions of anacrusic and crusic phrases.
- Teacher improvises crusic and anacrusic phrases. The students determine if the phrases are anacrusic or crusic and move to them. Teacher will tell the students to show energy in their movement for the anacrusis, and the arrival point of the crusis.
- Students practice individual crusic and anacrusic phrases in movement. These can be improvised phrases or phrases from a composed piece of music.
- Individual students perform a phrase, and the rest of the class determines which type of phrase it is.
- Teacher plays "Clowns" by Kabelevsky on the piano, and the students walk the beat and listen for anacrusic phrases.
- Teacher plays "Clowns" on the piano, and the students walk the beat and listen for anacrusic phrases. The students change direction for each phrase.
- Teacher plays "Clowns" on the piano, and the students walk the beat, change direction for each phrase and call out "anacrusic" or "crusic" as they change direction.
- Teacher plays "Clowns" again and has the students move to the melodic rhythm, focusing on the anacrusis and crusis.

78. Complementary Beats Reversal (video clip)

Concepts: Micro-beat, complementary rhythms

- Students stand in their self-spaces.
- On a hand drum, teacher plays an ostinato pattern. Students step that pattern.

- Teacher repeats the pattern, but asks the students to step only on the second beat of the half notes. Students step only on beat four of the first measure and beat two of the second measure.
- Divide students in half. One half of the class walks what they hear, the other half walks on the beats not played which are the complements.

Meaningful Movement: A Music Teacher's Guide to Dalcroze Eurhythmics

- Teacher keeps the original ostinato, but adds two more measures of any combination of quarter notes and half notes.
- Students learn to walk the four-measure pattern and then to walk the complements.

79. Complementary Rhythms - "The Happy Farmer"

Concept: Complementary rhythms

- Students stand in their self-spaces.
- Teacher plays "The Happy Farmer" by Schumann on the piano, and the students walk the beat.
- Teacher plays the piece, and the students walk and clap the beat.
- Teacher plays the piece, and the students clap the micro-beat (eighth notes).
- Teacher plays the piece, and the students clap the micro-beat and walk the beat.
- Teacher plays the melody only, and the students clap on the rests.
- Teacher plays the melody only, and the students walk the melodic rhythm.
- Teacher plays piece, and the students walk only on the rests.

80. Anapest/Dactylic Phrases

Concepts: Anapest/dactylic phrases, rhythmic patterns, quick reaction, differentiation

- Students stand in their self-spaces.
- Teacher improvises on the piano or uses a hand drum to play the anapest rhythm.

- Students walk the rhythm as the teacher continues to play the piano/hand drum.
- Teacher improvises on the piano or uses a hand drum to play the dactylic rhythm.

- Students walk the rhythm as the teacher continues to play the piano/hand drum.
- Teacher plays the anapest phrase for several measures and then changes to the dactylic phrase as the students are quickly reacting to the change.
- Repeat several times.
- This time when the teacher plays the phrases, the students walk the opposite phrase.

81. Shifting Accents with Racquetballs

Concept: Shifting accents

- Students stand in their self-spaces.
- Teacher distributes a racquetball to every student.
- Teacher taps the drum at 90 BPM in a meter of four and asks the students to bounce the ball on every beat one for four measures.
- Students bounce the ball only on beat two for the next four measures.
- Students bounce the ball only on beat three for the next four measures.
- Students bounce the ball only on beat four for the next four measures.
- Students do these four tasks continuously – bouncing the ball on beat one for four measures, beat two for four measures, beat three for four measures, and beat four for four measures for a total of sixteen measures.
- Students repeat the sequence, but only bounce the ball for two measures on each beat in an eight measure sequence - bouncing the ball on beat one for two measures, beat two for two measures, beat three for two measures, and beat four for two measures.
- Students repeat the sequence, but only bounce the ball for one measure on each beat in an four measure sequence - bouncing the ball on beat one for one measure, beat two for one measure, beat three for one measure, and beat four for one measure. Do this sequence twice for a total of eight measures. The challenge is to bounce the ball on beat four and immediately bounce the ball on beat one when beginning the sequence again.
- Students bounce the ball on beat one of the first measure, beat two of the second measure, beat three of the third measure, and beat four of the fourth measure. Repeat the sequence four times.
- Using "Bottom" by Zap Mama, bounce the ball on beat one of the second measure. From there, shift the accent one beat on every subsequent measure. Lead the students to discover that many of the bounces happen on the rests in the music.

82. Durations and Melodic Rhythm - "Ivan Sings"

Concepts: Whole note, half note, quarter note, phrasing, cooperative learning

- Students stand in their self-spaces.
- Teacher plays the first half of "Ivan Sings" by Khachaturian, and the students walk the beat.
- Teacher plays the first half again, and the students walk the half note.
- Teacher plays the first half again, and the students walk the whole note.
- Teacher plays the first half again, and the students walk to the melodic rhythm in an expressive manner.
- Students form pairs facing each other.
- Students put their left arms out with palms up and place the right hand fingertips on top of the partner's left hand.

- Teacher plays the first half of the piece and the students tap quarter, half, or whole notes as teacher indicates.
- Student "A" taps the beat and student "B" taps the melodic rhythm while the teacher plays the first half of the piece.
- Repeat the last step with the students switching tasks at the end of each phrase.

83. Measure by Measure Durations

Concepts: Quarter note, eighth note, eighth note triplet, sixteenth note, 4/4 meter, rhythmic improvisation

- Students stand in their self-spaces.
- Students walk four measures of various durations. Teach each measure separately, and then put them together.

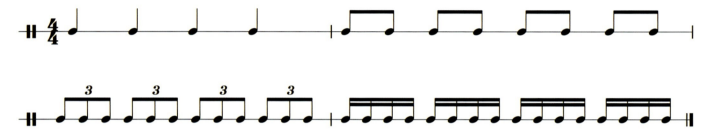

- Students form pairs and create a two-measure pattern using those rhythms.
- Students stand side by side, each holding the nearest shoulder and move to their compositions as the teacher plays the beat on the hand drum.
- One pair of "A" students teaches another pair of "B" students their pattern. The four students hold shoulders, and move to the following eight-measure (thirty-two beats) combination while teacher plays the beat on the hand drum:
  - ➢ "A" pattern (all move)
  - ➢ "B" pattern (all move)
  - ➢ "A" and "B" pattern together (each pair does their own at the same time)
  - ➢ Switch (each pair does the other's pattern at the same time)

84. Rhythmic Ostinato - Symphony #7, 2nd Movement

Concepts: Identifying and expressing motives, half note, quarter note, quarter rest

- Students stand in a circle.
- Teacher plays a pattern on the drum four times.

- Students step that pattern, moving in a circle.
- Teacher plays the variation of the pattern.

- Students express the pattern in mostly the upper body.
- Teacher writes the two patterns on the board and plays each pattern four times for students to practice.
- Teacher adds three more patterns found in the music. Students practice moving them expressively.

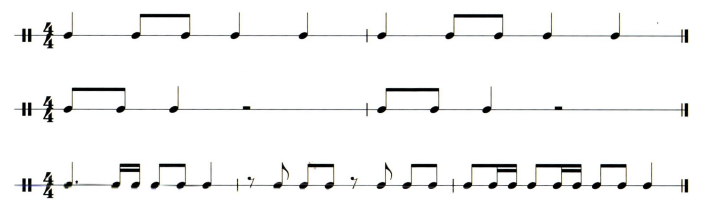

- Teacher hands out index cards containing the five patterns. Each student receives one card.
- Students move the pattern on the card for eight repetitions, then come to a circle to step the main pattern for four repetitions.
- On the fourth measure, students pass the cards behind them and break out of the circle to move the pattern on their new cards for eight repetitions.
- Add the music, Symphony #7, 2nd movement by Beethoven.

85. Rhythm Focus - "America" (video clip)

Concepts: Durations, rhythmic patterns, differentiation

- Students stand in their self-spaces.
- Students sing "America." (next page)

America
(My Country 'Tis of Thee)

Samuel Francis Smith Traditional

- Students sing the song while clapping the melodic rhythm.
- Students sing the song and clap on only the quarter notes that occur in "America."
- Students sing the song and walk on only the quarter notes.
- Students sing the song and walk on only the dotted eighth note/eighth note/quarter note combination.
- Repeat with different songs.
- Repeat with different note values.

86. Drumming Improvisation with Syncopation (video clip)

Concepts: Time, space and energy, rhythmic patterns, rondo, syncopation

- Students form pairs.
- Distribute one hand drum to each pair of students.
- The student holding the drum taps the drum on beat one in $\frac{4}{4}$.
- The student not holding the drum taps the drum on beat three. Student with the drum gives it to the partner and repeat.
- The student holding the drum walks the beat and taps the drum on beat one in $\frac{4}{4}$.
- The student not holding the drum needs to keep up with the drum holder and tap on beat three. Student with the drum gives it to the partner and repeat.
- The student holding the drum will always play on beat one.
- The student not holding the drum taps on the "and" of beat three.

Meaningful Movement: A Music Teacher's Guide to Dalcroze Eurhythmics

- The student not holding the drum taps on the "and" of beat two.
- The student not holding the drum taps on the "and" of two and the "and" of three.
- The student holding the drum taps on the "and" of four and on beat one.
- Combine the two, creating a pattern of the previous two rhythms.
- Each pair of students creates a four-beat pattern that includes syncopation.
- Make a drum circle to create a piece in rondo form where everyone plays for four measures, then four pairs of students play their patterns individually for four measures.

87. Syncopation - "Hello"

Concept: Syncopation

- Students stand in pairs facing each other. To form two parallel lines with the elastics, each student has an elastic and holds one end of the elastic wrapped around the wrist and holds the end of the partner's elastic wrapped around the other wrist. The students move the elastics to the beat while the teacher plays the chord progression of "Hello" by Adele in quarter notes.
- Students in pairs move the elastics to a rhythmic pattern while the teacher plays the chord progression of "Hello" in the syncopated rhythm.

- Students stand in their self-spaces and walk to the beat as the teacher plays the chord progression of "Hello."
- Students walk to the syncopation as the teacher plays the chords of "Hello."
- Play the recording of "Hello" - students are in pairs with elastics, showing the beat, then showing the syncopation, then individually walking to the beat, and finally walking to the rhythm of the syncopation as the teacher signals the beginning of each task.

88. Meter of Five - "Mission Impossible Theme"

Concept: Meter of five

- Students are seated on the floor, in pairs facing each other, about five feet apart.
- Teacher plays the beat in groups of five on the hand drum. The students roll the ball to each other - releasing on beat one and catching on beat five.
- Teachers plays "Mission Impossible Theme" by Elfman, and the students roll the ball to each other.
- Students stand in their self-spaces.
- Students walk five beats forward and change direction for the next five beats while the teacher plays the beat on the hand drum.
- Students walk on beat one of the five-beat grouping.
- Students walk on beats one, four, and five of the five-beat grouping.
- Teacher plays "Mission Impossible Theme" and students walk on beats one, four, and five of the five-beat grouping.

89. Meter of Five - "Take Five"

Concepts: Meter of five, macro-beat, micro-beat, accent

- Students stand in their self-spaces.
- Teacher repeatedly plays five micro-beats on the hand drum accenting beat one, and the students clap each beat and put an accent on beat one.
- Repeat last step but put micro-beats into two groups of 3+2, accenting beats one and four.
- Students sway on the macro-beats as they clap the micro-beats.
- Students sway and clap the macro-beats.
- Teacher demonstrates conducting an altered two pattern and the students conduct.
- Students conduct and walk the macro-beats.
- Add the music "Take Five" by Brubeck and have the students start by moving to the macro-beat and then eventually add the conducting pattern when the teacher indicates.

90. Meter of Seven - "Unsquare Dance"

Concepts: Meter of seven, macro-beat, micro-beat, accent

- Students stand in their self-spaces.
- Teacher repeatedly plays seven micro-beats on hand drum, accenting beat one, and the students follow by clapping all beats with the accent on beat one.
- Repeat previous step but group micro-beats into three macro-beats of 2+2+3.
- Students form pairs and pat right hands, pat left hands, pat both hands in the meter of seven with teacher playing on the hand drum. Pat on the micro-beats one, three, and five.
- Students perform the hand pat to "Unsquare Dance" by Brubeck.
- Students walk on the macro-beats as the teacher plays the hand drum.
- Teacher plays the "Unsquare Dance" recording, and the students begin by moving to the macro-beats. When the teacher cues them, the students find partners and perform the hand pat activity.

91. Mixed Meter - "All You Need is Love"

Concepts: Changing meters, form, conducting

- Students stand in their self-spaces.
- Teacher demonstrates meters of two, three, and four with conducting patterns.
- Students walk to the beat as the teacher plays "All You Need is Love" by McCartney.
- Students walk to the beat and change direction at the beginning of each section.
- Teacher asks students to identify the form - Intro, A (verse), A, B (chorus), A, B, A, B, B (fades out in the meter of four)
- Students conduct the meter patterns written on the board for each section.

Meaningful Movement: A Music Teacher's Guide to Dalcroze Eurhythmics

- Intro 4 4 4
- Verse 4 3 4 3 4 4 4 3
- Chorus 4 4 4 4 4 4 4 2

- Students conduct and walk the beat with the recording.

92. Mixed Meter - "In Freezing Winter"

Concepts: Anacrusis, crusis, and metacrusis, mixed meter

- Students stand in their self-spaces.
- Place the pattern of ||: 5 | 3 | 2 :|| on the board.
- Students pull imaginary threads from their elbows.
  - Longest thread is five and the shortest thread is two.
  - Emphasize the flow of the anacrusis, crusis, and metacrusis.
- Students form partners facing each other.
- Teacher plays the pattern above on a hand drum.
- Student "A" finds an imaginary thread on student "B" and pulls that thread off in five beats.
- Student "B" finds a thread on student "A" and pulls the thread off in three beats.
- Student "A" finds a thread on student "B" and pulls for two beats.
- Student "B" begins the pattern.
- Add to the pattern ||: 5 | 3 | 2 | 4 | 1 :||. Students face the teacher and pull imaginary threads from their own elbows following the new pattern.
- Students turn to their partners and alternate pulling the thread while the teacher plays the pattern on the hand drum.
- Allow groups of students to watch other groups to acquire new movement ideas.
- Students on their own walk the ||: 5 | 3 | 2 :|| pattern, taking one step for each beat.
- Teacher may play patterns on the drum or improvise on the piano.
- Change direction with each new measure using the anacrusis on the last beat.
- Go to the longer pattern and repeat the sequence. Energize the anacrusis.
- Using the longer pattern, the students step on beat one and gently tap the complements.
- Students repeat the longer pattern. They step on beat one and simultaneously pull a thread from themselves.
- Play the first two minutes of "In Freezing Winter Night" from *A Ceremony of Carols* by Britten and have the students repeat the last activity.

teacher tip

EMPHASIZE THE ANACRUSIS OR FORWARD MOTION OF THE HAND TOWARDS THE IMAGINARY THREAD. REMIND THE STUDENTS THAT THE THREADS EXIST IN MANY PLACES, NOT JUST IN THE SHOULDER AREA.

93. Mixed Meter - "Connla's Well"

Concept: Meter of seven (3 + 2 + 2)

- Students stand in their self-spaces.
- Teacher taps the drum for seven beats, accenting beat one.
- Students step only on beat one while tapping the micro-beats in their hands.
- Teacher taps the drum, accenting beats one, four and six.
- Students step on beats one, four and six while keeping the micro-beats in their hands.
- Students now step on beats one, four and six and tap the complements (when they are not stepping). ||: Step, tap, tap, step, tap, step, tap :||.
- Add the music, "Connla's Well" by Adiemus.
- Beginning: students listen to four phrases of seven before stepping on beat one and tapping the complements. Listen for four sequences of 3 + 2 at the 1:00.
- Repeat and have the students only step the macro-beats.
- Repeat and have the students only tap the complementary beats (two, three, five, seven)
- Divide class into two groups. One group steps the macro-beats, and the other group taps the micro-beats.

94. Overlapping and Continuous Canon (video clip)

Concepts: Overlapping and continuous canon, phrasing

a. Overlapping canon

- Students stand in pairs, facing each other, left hands holding the ends of one tie stretched between them, parallel to the ground.
- Teacher plays an eight-beat melody that is made up of an antecedent phrase followed by a consequent phrase, and then is followed by four beats of silence.
- Student "A" echoes the first four beat antecedent phrase by tapping and sliding a finger along the tie while student "B" is listening to the consequent phrase. Student "B" then echo-taps the consequent phrase during the four beats of silence.
- Repeat multiple times before asking student "B" to begin by tapping the antecedent phrase and student "A" to tap the consequent phrase.
- Individually, students step the eight-beat phrase four beats after the teacher. (see video)

b. Continuous canon

- Students stand in pairs, facing each other, left hands holding the ends of one tie stretched between them, parallel to the ground.
- Teacher plays an eight-measure melody of alternating antecedent and consequent phrases.

- Student "A" echo-taps the four antecedent phrases; student "B" echo-taps the four consequent phrases.
- Change the order so student "B" will echo-tap the antecedent phrases and student "A" will echo tap the consequent phrases.
- Individually, students stop the improvised melodies four beats behind the melody.

95. Melodic Rhythm and Canon - "Are You Sleeping?"

Concepts: Phrasing, melodic rhythm, interrupted and continuous canon, durations

- Students stand in their self-spaces.
- Students sing the song.

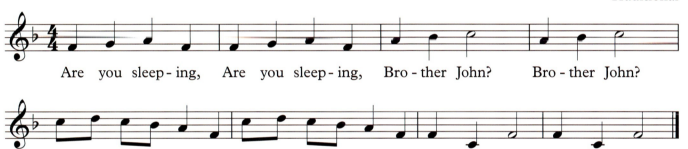

- Students sing the song while walking the beat.
- Students sing the song while clapping the melodic rhythm.
- Students sing the song while the teacher claps the melodic rhythm in canon (eight beats behind).
- Students sing the song while clapping the melodic rhythm in canon (eight beats behind).
- Students sing the song while clapping the melodic rhythm in canon but the clapping of the melodic rhythm is the first voice of the canon.
- Students sing the song while walking the melodic rhythm (eight beats behind).
- Students sing the song while walking the melodic rhythm in canon (eight beats behind).
- Students sing the song while walking the melodic rhythm in canon but the walking of the melodic rhythm is the first voice of the canon.
- Students divide into two groups and sing the song in canon.
- Students sing the song in canon in two groups, but each group also claps the melodic rhythm in canon, which creates a three-part canon.
- Students sing the song in canon in two groups, but each group also walks the melodic rhythm in canon, which creates a three-part canon.

96. Harmonic Dictation with I, IV, V7, vi (video clip)

Concepts: Major tonality, chord identification

- Students stand in their self-spaces.
- Teacher repeatedly plays a tonic (I) chord as quarter notes with the root in the bass. The students walk forward.
- Teacher repeatedly plays a dominant-seventh (V7) chord as quarter notes with the root in the bass. The students walk backwards.
- Teacher repeatedly plays a subdominant (IV) chord as quarter notes with the root in the bass. The students walk sideways.
- Teacher repeatedly plays a submediant (vi) chord as quarter notes with the root in the bass. Students walk in a circle.
- Teacher plays uneven phrases of the repeated chords, followed by various sequences of the four chords. The students walk in the corresponding directions.
- Teacher improvises a melody using the four chords. The students walk in the corresponding directions.

97. Cadence Dictation

Concepts: Full and half cadences

- Students stand in their self-spaces.
- Teacher plays a chordal sequence for eight beats in common time, ending on beat seven in a full cadence. Students walk the beat, and on beat eight, they stop walking and put their hands on their hips to represent the full cadence.
- Teacher plays a chordal sequence for eight beats in common time, ending on beat seven in a half cadence. Students walk the beat, and on beat eight, they stop walking and hold their hands up in a "V" shape to represent the half cadence.

98. Rhythmic Dictation - Minuet BMV 115

Concepts: Macro-beat, micro-beat, quarter note, dotted half note, anacrusis

- Students stand in their self-spaces.
- Teacher plays Minuet by Anna Magdelena Bach, and the students walk the macro-beat (dotted half note).
- Teacher plays Minuet, and the students walk the micro-beat (quarter note).
- Teacher plays Minuet, and the students walk the treble rhythm.
- Teacher plays Minuet, and the students walk the bass rhythm.
- Teacher plays Minuet, and half of the students walk the treble rhythm and half walk the bass rhythm.
- Switch tasks.
- Teacher cues the students to switch at different points during the piece of music.

Meaningful Movement: A Music Teacher's Guide to Dalcroze Eurhythmics

REMIND THE STUDENTS TO USE MORE ENERGY ON EACH ANACRUSIS.

99. Walking Bass/Clapping Treble (video clip)

Concepts: Pitch range recognition, durations, subdivision

- Students stand in their self-spaces.
- Teacher plays a melody of continuous quarter notes, eighth notes, half notes, or whole notes in the lower range of the piano, changing duration values every eight measures. The students show that note value in their feet, walking around the room.
- Teacher adds a melody of continuous durations in the upper range of the piano, but uses a different note value. Students clap this note value. Teacher can switch the note values played in either hand, including the use of rests. Students simultaneously walk and clap the played note values.
- The ratio can be 1:1, 2:1, 1:2, 4:1, or 1:4.

Advanced Phase

100. Polyrhythms - Two Against Three (video clip)

Concept: Polyrhythms

a. Three in the feet and two in the hands

- Students stand in their self-spaces.
- Teacher plays beat one of a three-beat pattern on the drum. Students subdivide the beat into three equal steps.
- Students continue walking and add a clap on beat one.
- Students continue to insert a second clap halfway between beat two and beat three.
- Teacher takes the pattern to the piano and plays three notes in the left hand against two notes in the right hand. Students put the two patterns together walking three beats and clapping two beats.

b. Two in the feet and three in the hands

- Students clap three beats in a circular motion.
- Students lift their dominant feet and lower them on beat one of the three pattern.
- Students insert the second step between beat two and three. Students should step backwards in order to keep the evenness between steps.
- Once students are comfortable with the pattern, they may step in any direction keeping three in the hands and two in the feet.
- Teacher improvises at the piano with three in the right hand and two in the left hand. Students put the two patterns together, walking two beats and clapping three beats.

Meaningful Movement: A Music Teacher's Guide to Dalcroze Eurhythmics

c. Shifting polyrhythms within the hands and feet
- From the piano, the teacher begins by playing a three-beat pattern in one hand. Students respond with clapping or stepping, depending on the register in which the teacher is playing.
- Teacher adds a two-beat pattern in the other hand, and the students add the clapping or stepping appropriate to the added register.
- Teacher stops playing the three-beat pattern so only the two-beat pattern is then being played. In that same register, the teacher switches from playing the two-beat pattern to playing the three-beat pattern. Then add the two-beat pattern in the other hand (register).

101. Polyrhythms - Five Against Two

Concept: Polyrhythms

- Follow the sequence for activity #100, making the necessary adjustments.

 **THE HALFWAY POINT OF THE FIVE PATTERN IS BETWEEN BEATS THREE AND FOUR.**

102. Polyrhythms - Three Against Two - "Après un Rêve"

Concept: Polyrhythms

- Students each take a necktie and face a partner, each one holding one end of both ties stretched in parallel lines.
- Teacher plays a slow beat on the hand drum and students move the ties forward and back showing three subdivisions.
- On the cue of "switch", students move the ties forward and back, showing two subdivisions. One pair of students crosses their ties over another pair of ties, creating a tic-tac-toe in the ties. Designate one pair as "A" and the other pair as "B".
- Pair "A" subdivides the beat into three, and pair "B" subdivides the beat into two.
- Switch on the teacher's cue.
- Using "Après un Rêve" by Fauré, one pair follows the piano (duple) and the other pair follows the melody, which switches between duple and triple.
- On the cue of "switch," the pairs switch tasks.

103. Durations, Melodic Rhythm, and Syncopation - "Ivan Sings"

Concepts: Whole note, half note, quarter note, syncopation, phrasing, expressive movement, cooperative learning

- Students stand in their self-spaces.

- Teacher plays the first half of "Ivan Sings" by Khachaturian, and the students walk the beat.
- Teacher repeats the first half of the piece and the students walk the half note.
- Teacher repeats the first half of the piece and the students walk the whole note.
- Teacher repeats the first half of the piece and the students walk to the melodic rhythm expressively.
- Students form pairs facing each other and designate one student as "A," and the other student as "B."
- Each student puts the left arm out with palm up and places the right hand fingertips on top of the partner's left hand.
- Teacher plays the first half of the piece, and the students tap quarter, half, or whole notes as the teacher indicates.
- The "A" student taps the beat and the "B" student taps the melodic rhythm while the teacher plays the first half of the piece.
- Repeat the previous step with the students switching tasks at the end of each phrase.
- Teacher plays the second half of the piece, and the students walk the beat and conduct a four pattern.
- Students clap the syncopated rhythm in the accompaniment.
- Students stand in pairs facing each other with one student designated as "A" and the other student designated as "B."
- Each student puts the left arm out with palm up and places the right hand fingertips on top of the partner's left hand.
- The "A" student taps the melodic rhythm, and the "B" student taps the accompaniment rhythm.
- Switch tasks.
- Teacher plays the second half of the piece and the students step to the accompaniment rhythm.
- Teacher plays the entire piece and asks the students to move to various durations, the melodic rhythm, and the accompaniment rhythm at different times.

104. Augmentation/Diminution

Concepts: Augmentation, diminution, expanding and contracting phrases

- Students stand in their self-spaces.
- Teacher writes a two-measure rhythmic phrase on the board.

- Students walk the phrase two times as the teacher improvises music to that rhythm.
- Teacher repeats the phrase two more times while the students stand in place and tap the rhythm on their drums.

- Students tap the phrase twice as fast (*hip*) four times. Teacher accompanies them through improvisation on the piano. Teacher writes out the new notation.

- Students tap the phrase twice as fast while the teacher plays the original phrase simultaneously.
- Students tap the original phrase two times followed by the new phrase twice as fast four times. Teacher plays the slower phrase throughout.
- Students tap the original phrase twice as slow. Teacher writes out the notation.

- Create a sequence of augmentation and diminution:
  - ➢ First phrase (twice)
  - ➢ Second phrase (four times)
  - ➢ First phrase (twice)
  - ➢ Third phrase (once)
- Students tap the sequence on the drums. Teacher maintains the original tempo throughout.

105. Meter of Seven - "Mikrokosmos" #33

Concepts: Meter of seven, creative movement, macro-beat, micro-beat

- Students stand in their self-spaces.
- Teacher plays "Mikrokosmos" #33 by Bartok, and the students move to the macro-beat.
- Students analyze the macro-beat pattern (2+2+3).
- Students move and conduct, elongating the third beat motion of the conducting pattern to the music.
- Students stand in circles of three. Each student is assigned to beat one, two, or three and each student claps the assigned individual macro-beat as the teacher plays the music.
- In the same circles, the student who claps on beat one decides how to clap the beat, and the other students must imitate the clap as the teacher plays the music.
- In the same circles, each student finds an individual way to show the beat as the teacher plays the music.
- In pairs, with elastics in parallel lines, the students move the elastics to the macro-beat as the teacher plays the music.

106. Meter of Nine - "Blue Rondo à la Turk"

Concepts: Meter of nine, macro-beat, micro-beat

- Students stand in their self-spaces.
- Teacher demonstrates conducting in nine/eight ("A" - 2+2+2+3 in an altered four pattern, elongating beat four) and the students conduct.
- Students conduct and walk the macro-beat as the teacher plays the hand drum or improvises on the piano.
- Teacher demonstrates conducting nine ("B"- 3+3+3 - in a traditional three pattern) and the students conduct.
- Students conduct and walk the macro-beat as teacher plays the hand drum or improvises on the piano.
- Students alternate between the two configurations of nine, conducting and walking the macro-beat.
- Students conduct and walk the macro-beat following this pattern - AAAB.
- Teacher plays "Blue Rondo à la Turk" by Brubeck, and the students conduct and walk the macro-beat (until 1:18 in the recording).
- Students form small groups and create movement to represent the meter patterns.
- Groups demonstrate their patterns for the rest of the class.

107. Changing the Meter of a Folk Song

Concepts: Meters, melodic rhythm, conducting

- Students stand in small groups.
- Each group selects a well known folk tune in simple meter.
- Each group changes the original meter to a meter of five or seven.
- Each group practices conducting and singing the piece in the changed meter.
- Each group practices walking the melodic rhythm.
- Each group demonstrates singing, walking, and conducting the song in the new meter for the class.

108. Groups of Twelve

Concepts: Division of twelve into twos, threes, fours, and sixes

- Students stand in their self-spaces.
- Teacher taps a rapid beat on the drum (BPM = 260), phrasing it in groups of twelve. Students take two steps within the twelve-beat phrases, stepping on beats one and seven.
- Teacher maintains the rapid beat and asks students to divide the twelve-beat pattern into three steps, or three groups of four.

- Students divide the twelve-beat pattern into four steps, or four groups of three.
- Students divide divide the twelve-beat pattern into six groups of two.
- Practice moving among sixes, fours, threes, and twos.
- Students create a pattern of sixes, fours, threes, and twos in any order. Each pattern must last for two groups of twelve. For example: four groups of six, twelve groups of two, six groups of four, eight groups of three. Students practice their individual patterns.
- Each person finds a partner. One student stands in place and observes the other student walking the individual pattern. The first student analyzes the movement, and tells the other student the order of patterns observed. Students switch tasks.
- Students individually create an ostinato that totals twelve beats. For example: six plus three plus three, or four plus four plus two plus two. Students practice the pattern.
- Each student finds a partner. Students take turns watching each other walk the ostinato four times. Students identify the partner's pattern.
- Play "Clapping Music" by Reich, and have students move through the space, experimenting with moving through sixes, fours, threes, and twos in any order while the teacher taps the beat.

109. Subdivision of the Macro-beat

Concepts: Macro-beat, micro-beat, subdivision

- Students stand in their self-spaces.
- Teacher plays a slow beat (BPM = 35). Students walk at that tempo for two beats. Then the students subdivide the beat and walk two steps per beat for two beats. Then they further subdivide the beat, and walk four steps per beat for two beats. Repeat the pattern several times. ||: 1 | 1 | 2 | 2 | 4 | 4 :||
- Students reverse the order of subdivisions, starting with four steps per beat, then two steps per beat, and then one step per beat. Repeat the pattern several times. ||: 4 | 4 | 2 | 2 | 1 | 1 :||
- Teacher plays the same slow beat on the hand drum. Students step the slow beat for two beats, then subdivide and walk three steps per beat for two beats. Then they further subdivide and walk six steps per beat for two beats. Repeat the pattern several times. ||: 1 | 1 | 3 | 3 | 6 | 6 :||
- Students reverse the order of subdivisions, starting with six steps per beat, then three steps per beat, and then one step per beat. Repeat the pattern several times. ||: 6 | 6 | 3 | 3| 1 | 1 :||
- Teacher writes this pattern on the board: ||: 1 | 1 | 2 | 2 | 3 | 3 | 4 | 4 | 5 | 5 | 6 | 6 :||. Students step the pattern, looking for particular challenges. Ask the students to speak "1, 2, 3, 4, 5" while stepping the subdivisions of five.
- Reverse the order of subdivisions – go from six down to one.
- Ask the students to create a logical order: ||: 1 | 1 | 4 | 4 | 2 | 2 | 6 | 6 | 3 | 3 | 5 | 5 :||, and walk the sequence they create.

- Distribute the score for "Psalm 23" by Rutter. Students follow the oboe line and step the micro-beats that range from one through five.
- Students follow the harp line, then the vocal line, and do the same.

TELL THE STUDENTS NOT TO WORRY ABOUT EXACTLY STEPPING THE FIVE AGAINST ONE.

110. Complementary Rhythms - "Scherzo on Tenth Avenue"

Concepts: Complementary rhythms, melodic rhythm, music memory

- Students stand in their self-spaces.
- Teacher plays "Scherzo on Tenth Avenue" by Kraehenbuehl, and the students walk the beat.
- Teacher plays the piece several times and the students walk the beat while starting to fill the rests with claps. Students stop walking when there are rests.
- Repeat the process with the students clapping the melodic rhythm and walking on the rests.
- Students stand in a double circle with the inside circle walking the melodic rhythm and clapping on the rests, and the outside circle walking the rests and clapping the melodic rhythm.
- Switch tasks.

111. Complementary Rhythms - "The Happy Farmer"

Concept: Complementary rhythms

- Students stand in their self-spaces.
- Teacher plays "The Happy Farmer" by Schumann on the piano, and the students walk the beat.
- Teacher plays the piece and the students walk and clap the beat.
- Teacher plays the piece and the students clap the micro-beat (eighth notes).
- Teacher plays the piece and the students clap the micro-beat and walk the beat.
- Teacher plays the melody only and the students clap on the complements (rests).
- Teacher plays the melody only and the students walk the melodic rhythm.
- Teacher plays the piece and the students walk on the complements (rests).
- Teacher plays the piece and the students walk the melodic rhythm and clap on the complements (rests).

112. Multi-Layered Rhythmic Reading

Concepts: Durations, conducting, rhythmic improvisation, literacy

- Students stand in their self-spaces.

- Students walk to the beat and conduct in $\frac{4}{4}$ while the teacher plays this chord progression on the piano: Cmaj7, Am7, Dm7, G7, Cmaj7, Am7, Dm7 (four beats each), then one measure of G7-Cmaj9 (eight measures).

- Students walk to the half notes and conduct while the teacher plays the chord progression.

- Students find a partner and stand one person in front of the other. The student in the back taps the beat on the partner's shoulders, and the student in front conducts as they both walk the beat while the teacher plays the chord progression.

- Students switch positions and tasks.

- Repeat the last activity, adding vocal rhythmic improvisation on "doo".

- Students face the board and speak the rhythm of line A (eight measures) on "doo," while walking in place to the beat. Teacher plays the chord progression as the students are speaking and walking in place. Practice until they know the rhythm well.

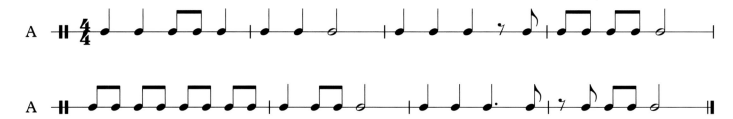

- Students face the board and clap line B (eight measures), while walking in place to the beat. Teacher plays the chord progression while they are clapping and walking in place. Practice until they know the rhythm well.

- Students combine rhythm A, rhythm B, and walking the beat. Teacher plays the chord progression as they are clapping and walking in place. Make sure that Line A is written directly above Line B on the board.

- The level of difficulty of lines A and B depends on the students' rhythmic skills and development.

GIVE THE STUDENTS THE OPPORTUNITY TO PRACTICE INDIVIDUALLY THE MEASURES THAT ARE DIFFICULT. *teacher tip*

113. Harmonic Dictation with i, iv, V7, VI

Concepts: Minor tonality, chord identification

- Students stand in their self-spaces.
- Teacher improvises a melody over a tonic (i) chord. Students walk forward to the beat.
- Teacher improvises a melody over a dominant-seven (V7) chord. Students walk backwards to the beat.
- Teacher improvises a melody over a subdominant (iv) chord. Students walk sideways to the beat.
- Teacher improvises a melody over a submediant (VI) chord. Students walk in a circle to the beat.
- Teacher plays uneven phrases of the repeated chords, followed by various sequences of the four chords. The students walk in the corresponding directions.
- Teacher improvises a melody using the four chords. The students walk in the corresponding directions.

114. Cadence Dictation

Concepts: Full, half, plagal, and deceptive cadences

- Students stand in their self-spaces.
- Teacher plays eight beats of chords in the following rhythm: six quarter notes with a half note ending in a full cadence. Students walk the beat, and on beat eight, they stop walking and put their hands on their hips to represent the full cadence.
- Teacher plays eight beats of chords in the following rhythm: six quarter notes with a half note ending in a half cadence. Students walk the beat, and on beat eight, they stop walking and hold their hands up in a "V" shape to represent the half cadence.
- Teacher plays eight beats of chords in the following rhythm: six quarter notes with a half note ending in a plagal cadence. Students walk the beat, and on beat eight, they stop walking and hold their hands down in a "V" shape to represent the plagal cadence.
- Teacher plays eight beats of chords in the following rhythm: six quarter notes with a half note ending in a deceptive cadence. Students walk the beat, and on beat eight, they stop walking and cross their arms, touching their shoulders to represent the deceptive cadence.

CHAPTER FOUR

EXPRESSIVE MOVEMENT/PLASTIQUE ANIMÉE
SHORT PROCESS/TEACHER-DRIVEN

Definition & Purpose

Plastique animée is defined as "an artistic and creative embodiment of the music through individual or group movement." It is an expressive visualization of the music in an artistic and meaningful way. The exploration activities provide a foundation for the more advanced expressive movement activities. These activities are typically done within one class period indicating a short process, and have a structure provided by the teacher, thus, teacher-driven. Once the students have had opportunities to move creatively and expressively through these activities, they will be ready to participate in the long process/student-driven plastique animée experiences found at the end of the chapter.

EXPRESSIVE MOVEMENT/ PLASTIQUE ANIMÉE
SHORT PROCESS/TEACHER-DRIVEN
Chart of Activities

INTRODUCTORY	BEGINNING	INTERMEDIATE	ADVANCED
115. Movement Exploration – Direction	123. Movement Exploration - Energy/Articulation Gestures	129. Conducting for Nuance - "Il Deserto"	136. Syncopation - "Let it Go"
116. Movement Exploration - Pitch Range Levels	124. Exploration with Half Notes -"Recordare"	130. Diamond Shadowing in Quartets - "Luminosa"	137. Syncopation - "Oblivion"
117. Movement Exploration - Energy/Dynamics	125. Exploration with Whole Notes - "Baba Yetu"	131. Flocking - "Brandenburg Concerto #6, 1st Mvt."	138. Mixed Meter - "Knee I"
118. Movement Exploration - *Legato*/Flow	126. Consonance/Dissonance Circle	132. Micro-Beats and Macro-Beats - "Devil's Beauties"	139. Tension and Relaxation -"Miserere"
119. Movement Exploration - Energy/Weight Articulation	127. Mirroring - "Song for Viola"	133. Tension and Release with Elastics - "Hymn Do Trójcy Świętej"	140. Abstract Space
120. Mirroring	128. Shadowing - "Moonlight Sonata"	134. Consonance/Dissonance Circle - "Voca Me"	
121. Statues - "Gabriel's Oboe"		135. Meter of Six - "Dream is Collapsing"	
122. Story Re-Enactment			

Meaningful Movement: A Music Teacher's Guide to Dalcroze Eurhythmics

EXPRESSIVE MOVEMENT/PLASTIQUE ANIMÉE
SHORT PROCESS/TEACHER-DRIVEN

Sample Lesson Plan with Assessment

"STATUES"

Introductory Phase

Objectives:

1. The student will demonstrate flow.
2. The student will show creative movements appropriate to the music.
3. The student will interact in a small group.

National Standards:

Creating, Performing, and Responding

Materials:

- "Gabriel's Oboe" from The Mission by Ennio Morricone
- Finger cymbals

Procedure:

1. Students stand in circles of five or six.
2. One student is in the middle of the circle and strikes a pose and the teacher begins the music "Gabriel's Oboe" by Morricone.
3. Teacher plays finger cymbals and another student joins the circle, striking a pose that is complementary to the first pose.
4. The process continues until all students are part of the statue.
5. When the teacher says "flow," the students slowly flow to another position.
6. When the teacher says "freeze," the students stop flowing.
7. This process continues throughout the music.
8. The teacher encourages students to use different levels and be creative in their statue positions.

Assessment:

1. The teacher will observe flow in the students' movements.
2. The teacher will observe the creative movements appropriate to the music.
3. The teacher will listen to the students as they reflect on the success of being part of a group.

Meaningful Movement: A Music Teacher's Guide to Dalcroze Eurhythmics

EXPRESSIVE MOVEMENT/ PLASTIQUE ANIMÉE
SHORT PROCESS/TEACHER-DRIVEN:
Statues Rubric

	UNSATISFACTORY	PROGRESSING	SATISFACTORY	OUTSTANDING
Flow	Does not demonstrate continuous movement between statue positions.	Inconsistently demonstrates continuous movement between statue positions.	Usually demonstrates continuous movement between statue positions.	Always demonstrates continuous movement between statue positions.
Creative Movements	The quality of the movement does not reflect the quality of the music.	The quality of the movement inconsistently reflects the quality of the music.	The quality of the movement usually reflects the quality of the music.	The quality of the movement always reflects the quality of the music, and creates poses that are complementary to the group statue.
Social Interaction	Does not interact with the group in an appropriate way.	Inconsistently interacts with the group in an appropriate way.	Usually interacts with the group in an appropriate way.	Always interacts with the group in an appropriate way.

EXPRESSIVE MOVEMENT/PLASTIQUE ANIMÉE
SHORT PROCESS/TEACHER-DRIVEN

Description of Activities

Introductory Phase

115. Movement Exploration - Direction

Concepts: Steady beat, directional paths, shapes

- Students stand in their self-spaces.
- Teacher plays the beat on a hand drum and gives directional paths for the students to move. Students will have to negotiate the space to keep from running into other students, walls, or items in the room.

  - ➢ Forward
  - ➢ Backwards
  - ➢ Sideways
  - ➢ Diagonal
  - ➢ Zig-zag
  - ➢ Square
  - ➢ Large circle
  - ➢ Small circle
  - ➢ Rectangle
  - ➢ Triangle

Meaningful Movement: A Music Teacher's Guide to Dalcroze Eurhythmics

116. Movement Exploration - Pitch Range Levels

Concepts: Steady beat, pitch ranges, movement in levels exploration

- Students stand in their self-spaces.
- When the students hear the music in a high range on the piano (improvised by the teacher), they move to the beat while standing tall with their hands up in the air.
- When the students hear music in a medium or low range on the piano, they move in a lower level according to the music.
- Students can choose directional paths to move and will have to negotiate the space to keep from running into other students, walls, or items in the room.

117. Movement Exploration - Energy/Dynamics

Concepts: Steady beat, dynamics, use of energy exploration

- Students stand in their self-spaces.
- When the students hear music at a *forte* level on the piano (improvised by the teacher), they move to the beat and show the energy of the music with their movements.
- When the students hear music at a *piano* level, they adjust the size and energy of their movements.
- Students can choose directional paths to move and will have to negotiate the space to keep from running into other students, walls, or items in the room.

118. Movement Exploration - *Legato*/Flow

Concepts: *Legato*, continuous motion exploration

- Students stand in their self-spaces.
- When the students hear *legato* music either improvised on the piano or from a recording, they move to the beat and show flow with their bodies.
- Students should initiate the continuous motion with various parts of their bodies.
- Students can choose directional paths to move and will have to negotiate the space to keep from running into other students, walls, or items in the room.
- Students can also demonstrate *legato* with non-locomotor movement.

119. Movement Exploration - Energy/ Weight Articulation

Concepts: Steady beat, *marcato* and *staccato* articulation, use of energy exploration

- Students stand in their self-spaces.
- When the students hear *marcato* music on the piano (improvised by the teacher), they move to the beat and show the energy of the articulation with strong movements.

- When the students hear *staccato* music, they show the energy of the articulation with quick and sharp movements.
- Students can choose directional paths to move and will have to negotiate the space to keep from running into other students, walls, or items in the room.
- Students can also demonstrate *marcato* and *staccato* with non-locomotor movement.

120. Mirroring

Concepts: *Legato*, phrasing, body exploration, cooperative learning

- Students stand in pairs facing each other.
- Student "A" student starts by moving a part/parts of the body in a flowing manner for eight beats (teacher is either playing the drum or improvising on the piano) and student "B" mirrors the movement (split-second imitation).
- Student "B" leads the next eight beats.
- They continue the process of student "A" leading for eight beats, then student "B" leading for eight beats throughout the music.

> **teacher tip**
> ENCOURAGE THE STUDENTS TO BE CREATIVE AND TO INITIATE THE MOVEMENTS WITH VARIOUS PARTS OF THEIR BODIES.

121. Statues

Concepts: *Legato*, body exploration, creative movement, cooperative learning

- Students stand in circles of five or six.
- One student is in the middle of the circle and strikes a pose. The teacher begins the music "Gabriel's Oboe" by Morricone.
- Teacher plays finger cymbals and another student joins the circle, striking a pose that is complementary to the first pose.
- The process continues until all students are part of the statue.
- When the teacher says "flow," the students slowly flow to another position.
- When the teacher says "freeze," the students stop flowing.
- The process continues to the end of the piece.

Students demonstrate the concept of Statues.

> **teacher tip**
> ENCOURAGE THE STUDENTS TO USE DIFFERENT LEVELS IN THEIR POSITIONS.

122. Story Re-enactment

Concept: Creative movement

- Students sit in front of the teacher on the floor.
- "Jump, Frog, Jump" by Robert Kalan
    - Read the story and ask students to jump whenever they hear the words, "jump, frog, jump."
    - Repeat the story, adding piano accompaniment to the phrase, "jump, frog, jump."

    - Discuss why the accompaniment sounded appropriate (short, syllabic matching, high in range).
- Read "The Bunnies are Not in Their Beds" by Marisabina Russo (or create your own story). Have the students act out what is happening in the story based on musical cues the teacher plays on the piano. The music the teacher improvises for the story establishes the type of movement the students do.

Beginning Phase

123. Movement Exploration - Energy/Articulation Gestures

Concepts: *Marcato, staccato, legato* articulations, gestures exploration

- Students stand in their self-spaces. These activities are non-locomotor.
- Teacher improvises on the piano and the students show the following gestures using a variety of body parts.
    - Push (*marcato*)
    - Pull (*marcato*)
    - Dab (*marcato*)
    - Flick (*staccato*)
    - Punch (*marcato*)
    - Bend (*legato*)
    - Twist (*legato*)
    - Swing (*legato*)
    - Stretch (*legato*)

124. Exploration with Half Notes - "Recordare"

Concepts: Half notes, *legato*, steady beat, dynamics, creative movement, cooperative learning

- Students stand in pairs facing each other and form two parallel lines. Each student has an elastic and holds one end of the elastic wrapped around the wrist and holds the end of the partner's elastic wrapped around the other wrist.
- When the music, "Recordare" by Libera is played, the students move the elastics to the half notes in creative ways reflecting the dynamics.

Students demonstrate Exploration with Whole Notes using elastics.

125. Exploration with Whole Notes - "Baba Yetu"

Concepts: Whole notes, *legato*, steady beat, dynamics, creative movement, cooperative learning

- Students stand in their self-spaces.
- Each student holds an elastic.
- While the teacher plays the beat on a hand drum, the students move through space, stepping the quarter note beat while stretching the material for four beats (whole note).
- When the teacher says "small group," the students will get into small groups and join elastics together and continue to stretch the whole notes in an expressive way.
- When the teachers says "large group," the students get into large groups and join the elastics together and continue to stretch the whole notes in an expressive way.
- Repeat this activity using the music "Baba Yetu" by Tin. Student movement with the elastics should also reflect the dynamics in this piece.

126. Consonance/Dissonance Circle

Concepts: Consonance, dissonance, cooperative learning

- Students stand in a large circle with their arms out to the side, palms outward touching their neighbors' palms.
- Teacher improvises atonal music mixing consonant and dissonant passages. A recording can be used as well. When the music becomes dissonant, the students push out through their palms into their neighbors' palms. When the music is consonant, the palms relax.

Students demonstrate Consonance/Dissonance.

Meaningful Movement: A Music Teacher's Guide to Dalcroze Eurhythmics

127. Mirroring - "Song for Viola"

Concepts: *Legato*, phrasing, body exploration, cooperative learning

- Students stand in pairs facing each other.
- Student "A" starts out by moving the body in a flowing manner for eight beats (teacher is either playing the drum or improvising on the piano) and student "B" mirrors the movement (split-second imitation).
- Student "B" leads the next eight beats.
- They continue to alternate who is leading the movement.
- Repeat the activity with "Song for Viola" by Adams. This piece is in a slow 12/8 so each phrase will be twelve beats long.
- All of the movement is non-locomotor.

 **ENCOURAGE STUDENTS TO BE CREATIVE AND TO INITIATE THE MOVEMENTS WITH VARIOUS PARTS OF THEIR BODIES.**

128. Shadowing - "Moonlight Sonata"

Concepts: *Legato*, phrasing, body exploration, cooperative learning

- Students stand in pairs, one student standing in front, not facing the other student.
- Student "A" (in front) moves in a flowing manner and student "B" (behind) imitates the movement.
- Student "A" turns half way around indicating that student "B" should now turn half way around and lead.
- Add the music, "Moonlight Sonata" by Beethoven.

Intermediate Phase

129. Conducting for Nuance

Concepts: Meter of four, nuance, dynamics, *rubato*, expression

- Students stand in their self-spaces.
- Using "Il deserto" by Morricone, the students conduct a four pattern, showing the nuance in tempo and dynamics in their patterns.

130. Diamond Shadowing in Quartets - "Luminos" (video clip - music is improvised)

Concepts: *Legato*, phrasing, body exploration, expressive movement, cooperative learning

- Students stand in groups of four or five and form a diamond or star shape.
- One student is the head of the group and faces outward. The rest of the students face in the same direction as the head student.

Meaningful Movement: A Music Teacher's Guide to Dalcroze Eurhythmics

- When the music, "Luminos" by Libera is played, the lead student moves in a flowing, expressive manner to the music. The other students mirror the movement using split second imitation.
- After leading for a few phrases, the lead student turns one to the right, indicating that that student should now lead the movement. All students are now facing the same direction as the new leader.
- Repeat these steps until the music ends.

131. Flocking - "Brandenburg Concerto #6," 1st Movement

Concepts: Expressive movement, cooperative learning

- Students stand in groups of three, in a triangle formation.
- When Bach's *Brandenburg Concerto #6*, 1st movement is played, the students move through the room expressively, led by the student at the top of the triangle. Students periodically follow another student, mirroring the leader's movement.
- Students continually form different size groups throughout the piece, and a student within that group leads and then can pass on the lead to someone by nodding the head to a student on either side.
- Students can move individually.
- All of the movement is loco-motor.

132. Micro-Beats and Macro-Beats - "Devil's Beauties"

Concepts: Micro-beat, macro-beat, articulation

- Students stand in their self-spaces.
- Teacher lightly taps a steady beat (MM = 225) on a hand drum. Students show the tempo lightly by clapping in a circle over four beats with two fingers.
- Students maintain the tapping at 225, but take one step for every four taps.
- Students maintain the tapping, but take one step for every eight taps.
- Students eliminate the tapping, but take macro-steps 1:4 or 1:8 on the teacher's cue.
- Students listen to a recording of "The Devil's Beauties" by Dompierre.
- The class is divided in half: one half creates movement in response to the *pizzicato* line and the other half creates movement in response to the *legato* lines.

133. Tension and Relaxation - "Hymn Do Trójcy Świętej"

Concepts: Tension and relaxation, cooperative learning

- Students stand in their self-spaces. Each student has an elastic.
- Students work individually to increase and release tension in their elastics over various phrase lengths in response to the teacher's playing on the hand drum or piano. Teacher asks everyone to breathe, inhaling when the tension is increasing and exhaling when the tension is releasing.

Students create tension in the elastics.

- Students work in pairs to increase and release tension in the elastics.
- Students work in quartets to increase and release tension in the elastics.
- Diagram the music, "Hymn Do Trójcy Świętej" by Tin on the board and ask the students to perform the expressive movement:
  - ➢ **0:00 minutes**: Individually, increase and release tension in response to the music.
  - ➢ **2:20 minutes**: Students combine in small groups, connecting their elastics, to show the tension and release in the music.
  - ➢ **4:50 minutes**: Drop the elastics to the floor and express the tension and relaxation individually or in groups using only their bodies.

134. Consonance/Dissonance Circle - "Voca Me"

Concepts: Consonance, dissonance, macro-beat, cooperative learning

- Students stand in a large circle with their arms out to the side, palms outward touching their neighbors' palms.
- Teacher plays atonal music mixing consonant and dissonant passages. When the music becomes dissonant, the students push out through their palms into their neighbors' palms. When the music is consonant, the palms relax.
- Using the piece, "Voca Me," by Libera, students push their palms out when they hear dissonance while walking in place to the macro-beat.
- During the solo section the students break from the group and walk the macro-beat.
- When the teacher cues "small group," the students form small group circles, and push out during the dissonance.

135. Meter of Six - "Dream is Collapsing"

Concepts: Meter of six, macro-beat, micro-beat, *ritardando*, rhythmic pattern

- Students stand in pairs, facing each other with elastics in parallel lines.
- Students move the elastics to the macro-beat (dotted half note) as the teacher improvises on the piano or plays the hand drum.
- Students move to the macro-beat to the first half of the recording, "Dream is Collapsing" (stop at the *ritardando*).
- Teacher improvises or plays a hand drum to the pattern quarter/half note (slow tempo) and the students, in pairs, move the elastics to the pattern.

- Start the recording after the ritardando, and ask the students to use the elastics to move to that rhythm pattern.
- Play the recording:
  - ➤ Students start in their self-spaces and move to the macro-beat. Students reflect the dynamic levels in their movement.
  - ➤ When the teacher cues "partners," the students find partners and move the elastics to the macro-beat until the end of the *ritardando*.
  - ➤ After the *ritardando*, the partners move the elastics to the quarter/half note rhythmic pattern.
  - ➤ When teacher cues "break," the students individually walk to the rhythmic pattern.

Advanced Phase

136. Syncopation - "Let it Go"

Concepts: Macro-beat, micro-beat, syncopation

- Students stand in their self-spaces.
- Students clap a pattern.

- Students walk the pattern.
- Students walk the pattern with the music, "Let it Go" five times, and then walk eight half notes (macro-beats): 0:00-0:42.
- Students listen to the bridge section of "Let it Go" and tap the beat lightly on any part of the body: 2:33-2:54.
- Students listen to the bridge section again and tap the syncopated melodic rhythm lightly on any part of the body.
- In pairs, one student taps the beat while the other student taps the syncopated melodic rhythm, both in each others' palms while listening to the bridge section.
- Switch tasks.
- "Let it Go" by Lopez
  - ➤ During the introduction and first half of the first verse, the students walk the syncopated pattern five times, and then walk eight half notes (macro-beats): 0:00-0:42.
  - ➤ Students walk the macro-beat until the chorus starts: 0:42-0:59.
  - ➤ At the beginning of the chorus, the students show the whole notes with arm movements while walking the macro-beat.

- ➤ Students show the syncopation in the melodic rhythm at the end of the chorus with their feet and arms: 0:59-1:13.
- ➤ Students pat the melodic rhythm of the last phrase: 1:13-1:27.
- ➤ Students walk the micro-beat: 1:27-1:45.
- ➤ Students walk the macro-beat: 1:45-2:01.
- ➤ In the next chorus section, the students show the whole notes with arm movements while walking the macro-beat: 2:01-2:15.
- ➤ Students walk the syncopated melodic rhythm: 2:15-2:25.
- ➤ During the sixteen-beat transition, the students move towards a partner: 2:25-2:33.
- ➤ During this section with the students being in pairs, one student taps the beat, and the other student taps the syncopated melodic rhythm, both in each others' palms: 2:33-2:54.
- ➤ At the end of that section both students pat the macro-beat in each others' hands ("high five") five times: 2:54-3:02.
- ➤ In the final chorus section, the students show the whole notes with arm movements while walking the macro-beat: 3:02-3:16.
- ➤ Students walk the syncopated melodic rhythm: 3:16-3:30.
- ➤ At the end of the song, the students pat the melodic rhythm: 3:30-3:32.

137. Syncopation - "Oblivion"

Concepts: Syncopation, expressive movement

- Students stand in pairs with elastics in parallel lines, and move to the syncopated rhythm.

- Add the music, "Oblivion," by Piazzolla and continue that movement.
- Students individually show the syncopated rhythm in their feet and use their hands to move the elastics in an arch to show four beats while the teacher plays the rhythm on the hand drum.
- Add the recording.
- Play the music again starting with the individual movement. When the teacher cues "partners," the students pair up and move the elastics to the syncopated rhythm.

138. Mixed Meter - "Knee I"

Concepts: Time, space, and energy, mixed meter

- Students stand in pairs.
- Teacher writes a pattern of ||: 4 | 6 | 8 :|| on the board.

- Student "A" creates a four-beat gesture, such as lifting an elbow.
- Student "B" expands the gesture to six beats, using more space.
- Student "A" expands the gesture to twice the number of beats of the original gesture.
- Student "B" begins a new four-beat gesture. Continue the sequence.
- Students remember who their partners are, but walk away from them.
- Students turn towards their partners and repeat the ||: 4 | 6 | 8 :|| sequence from a distance.
- Using "Knee I" by Glass, students create an A-B-A form. For the A section, students step on beat one of each measure in the ||: 4 | 6 | 8 :|| sequence and flow through the rest of the measure.
- After approximately eight sequences, the teacher calls out "partner." Students stop where they are and visually locate their partners. Students stand in place and create expanded gestures with their partners, still following the ||: 4 | 6 | 8 :|| pattern.
- After approximately eight sequences, teacher cues "on your own," and students resume stepping on beat one of each measure in the sequence and flowing through the rest of the measure.

139. Tension and Relaxation - "Miserere"

Concepts: Tension and relaxation

- Students stand in their self-spaces. Each student has an elastic.
- During the plainchant, the students step around the room demonstrating the long phrases by changing direction and/or movement.
- Students link elastics with one other student. During the choral section, the students express the music in non-locomotor movement.
- When the choral section ends, the students disconnect the elastics and move individually to the plainchant phrase rhythm, finding a new partner. Link the elastic with another student when the choral section resumes.

140. Abstract Space (video clip)

Concepts: Exploring space, cooperative learning, creative movement

- Students stand in pairs and manipulate horizontal space. Experiment with no pulse and then put in eight-beat phrases. Change leaders.
  - Mirror (follow)
  - Circus mirror (split second imitation)
  - Magnet (split second imitation and cross into each other's space)
  - Opposite magnet

CHAPTER FOUR PART 2

EXPRESSIVE MOVEMENT/PLASTIQUE ANIMÉE
LONG PROCESS/STUDENT-CREATED

Plastique animée is most often developed over several class periods, indicating a longer process. It should be created by the students with minimal teacher input. After becoming familiar with the music, the teacher helps the students to identify key musical concepts on which to focus their movement in purposeful, artistic, and creative ways. The predominant musical concepts of each piece are provided in the following chart.

EXPRESSIVE MOVEMENT/PLASTIQUE ANIMÉE
LONG PROCESS/STUDENT-CREATED

Music Chart with Concepts

INTRODUCTORY	BEGINNING	INTERMEDIATE	ADVANCED
141. "Aquarium" *Carnival of the Animals*, Saint-Saëns • *legato* • step-wise motion • melodic contour	144. "Fossils" *Carnival of the Animals*, Saint-Saëns • steady beat • rhythmic patterns	149. "Baba Yetu" Tin • steady beat • dynamics • rhythmic patterns • voices	155. "Adagio for Strings" Barber • dynamics • tension/relaxation • consonance/dissonance nuance
142. "Elephants" *Carnival of the Animals*, Saint-Saëns • triple meter • piano/double bass • *legato/staccato*	145. "Gabriel's Oboe" *The Mission*, Morricone • *rubato* • *legato* • nuance	150. "Cider House Rules Main Theme" Portman • triple meter • phrasing • *legato* • nuance	156. "Mille echi" *La Piovra*, Morricone • compound meter • *legato/staccato* • polyrhythms • nuance
143. "Kangaroos" *Carnival of the Animals*, Saint-Saëns • *staccato/legato* • high/low	146. "Lumos!" *Harry Potter and the Prisoner of Azkaban*, Williams • steady beat • dynamics • compound meter • articulations	151. "Flying Theme" (E.T.), Williams • skips • triple meter • *legato* • *ritardando* • *rubato*	157. "Lacrymosa" *Requiem*, Mozart • dynamics • compound meter • articulations • nuance • voices
	147. "O Fortuna" *Carmina Burana*, Orff • dynamics • rhythmic patterns • voices	152. "Jurassic Park Theme" Williams • melodic contour • *legato* • phrasing • nuance	158. "Tango Sensations: Fear" Piazzolla • ternary form • dynamics • articulation • rhythmic patterns • nuance

EXPRESSIVE MOVEMENT/ PLASTIQUE ANIMÉE LONG PROCESS/STUDENT-CREATED

Music Chart with Concepts, continued

BEGINNING	INTERMEDIATE	ADVANCED
148. "Swan" *Carnival of the Animals,* Saint-Saëns • *legato* • melodic contour • harp/cello	153. "Romeo and Juliet" Prokofiev • dotted eighth/sixteenth note rhythm • eighth notes	159. "Nimrod", *Enigma Variations,* Elgar • dynamics • consonance/dissonance • nuance
	154. "Superman Theme" Williams • triplets • accents • dynamics • rondo	160. "Oblivion" Piazzolla • syncopation • dynamics • *rubato* • nuance
		161. "Pavanne" Fauré • *legato/staccato* • *rubato* • phrasing • nuance
		162. "Sand" Lanier • dynamics • articulations • nuance
		163. "The Lady Caliph: Nocturne" Morricone • *rubato* • dynamics • *legato* • phrasing • piano/strings • nuance
		164. "Unstoppable" Posthumus • dynamics • articulations • rhythmic patterns • nuance

CHAPTER FIVE

RHYTHMIC SOLFÈGE *Definition & Purpose*

Rhythmic solfège is an aspect of the Dalcroze approach that focuses on purposeful movement while singing; the creation and manipulation of melodies; and the strengthening of inner hearing in both rhythm and pitch. Rhythmic solfège includes diatonic scales and modes, stressing the position of the semi-tones within space and time. While modifications can be made for teachers who use a pentatonic scale in the early grades, exposing students to diatonic music early is an important goal. While rhythmic solfège is often taught using a fixed-*do* approach where the pitch "C" always is *do*, music educators in the countries that use a moveable-*do* approach can easily adapt the lessons to their curriculum.

RHYTHMIC SOLFÈGE Chart of Activities

INTRODUCTORY	BEGINNING	INTERMEDIATE	ADVANCED
165. Melodic Hopscotch	168. Tonal Distraction	177. Invitation to "*Do*"	196. Snapping High/Clapping Low
166. Snapping High/Clapping Low	169. Gravity Scale	178. Tonal Distraction	197. Major/Minor Scale Quick Reaction
167. Solfège Dictation	170. Melodic Hopscotch	179. Gravity Scale	198. Major/Minor Scale in Solfège/Numbers/Letter Names
	171. Snapping High/Clapping Low	180. "*Do*" is Home	199. Major/Minor Scale in Meters/Rhythmic Patterns with Syncopation
	172. Fly Back Home	181. Find Your "*Do*"	200. Additive Major/Minor Scale
	173. Major Scale Quick Reaction	182. Scales with *hip* and *hop*	201. Turn Ornamentation
	174. Dichords	183. Major Scale - Half/Whole Steps	202. Fragmented Song/Solfège
	175. Tone Row Manipulation	184. Major Scale Inner Hearing	203. Sight-Reading in Canon - "Water Canon"
	176. Solfège Dictation	185. Major Scale in Solfège/Numbers/Letter Names	204. Tone Row Manipulation
		186. Major Scale in Meters/Rhythmic Patterns	205. Solfège Dictation
		187. Additive Major Scale	206. Melodic/Rhythmic Dictation - Non-Familiar Song

RHYTHMIC SOLFÈGE
Chart of Activities, continued

INTERMEDIATE
188. Trichords
189. Trill Ornamentation
190. Snapping High/ Clapping Low
191. Fragmented Solfège
192. Tone Row Manipulation
193. "The Ghost of John"
194. Melodic/Rhythmic Dictation - Familiar
195. Solfège Dictation

RHYTHMIC SOLFÈGE

Sample Lesson Plan with Assessment

"TONE ROW MANIPULATION"

Intermediate Phase

Objectives:
1. The student will demonstrate a diatonic tone row vocally and moving through space.
2. The student will demonstrate the ability to manipulate the row through various musical approaches.

National Standards:
Creating and Responding

Materials:
Space for movement, board with staff lines, nine-measure tone row.

Procedure:

1. Students stand on their pre-assigned low *do* spots in their self-spaces, facing the board and step and sing a *do* to *do* scale forward and backwards.

2. Students step and sing the row on the board, filling in the missing intervals.

3. Students step and sing the row in retrograde, filling in the missing intervals.

4. Students are divided into two groups - one group steps and sings the row forward and one group steps and sings the row in retrograde.

5. Both groups step and sing the row forward, but the second group begins four measures after the first group begins (canon).

6. Both groups step and sing the row in retrograde, but the second group begins four measures after the first group begins (canon).

7. Students are divided into four groups:
   a. Group 1 - performs the original row
   b. Group 2 - performs the original row in canon
   c. Group 3 - performs the row in retrograde
   d. Group 4 - performs the row in retrograde canon

Assessment:

1. The teacher will observe the student's ability to sing and step the rhythm of the row.
2. The teacher will observe the flow of the students' movements relative to their singing.
3. The teacher will observe the aural and physical independence of the student in group work.

SOLFÈGE: Tone Row Manipulation Rubric

	UNSATISFACTORY	PROGRESSING	SATISFACTORY	OUTSTANDING
Vocal Production	Does not match correct pitches from the board to the solfège syllables.	Interprets half of the row correctly with correct solfège names and pitches.	Interprets most of the row with correct solfège names and pitches.	Accurately interprets the row with the correct solfège names and pitches.
Stepping the Row	Does not match the steps to the melodic contour of the row.	Matches some steps to the melodic contour of the row. Does not demonstrate intervals of 2nds or 3rds.	Matches all steps to the melodic contour of the row. Does not accurately demonstrate intervals of 2nds or 3rds.	Matches all steps to the melodic contour of the row and accurately demonstrates intervals of 2nds and 3rds.
Vocal and Movement Independence	Does not demonstrate vocal and movement independence.	Begins a phrase independently, but loses the melodic contour of the row by measure four.	Demonstrates partial independence with the support of student peers.	Demonstrates independence of parts and leadership when in small groups.

RHYTHMIC SOLFÈGE *Description of Activities*

> **"C" IS ALWAYS *DO* UNLESS INDICATED OTHERWISE.**
> **THIS ELIMINATES THE FIXED *DO* AND MOVABLE *DO* QUESTION.** — *teacher tip*

Introductory Phase

165. Melodic Hopscotch

Concept: Same/different

- Students stand in their self-spaces.
- Teacher plays three different pitches on the piano.
- Teacher plays three pitches a second time, altering one of the pitches.
- Teacher plays the second set of three pitches (with the one altered pitch) and the students hop on one foot for the same pitch and jump on two feet for the altered pitch as the teacher plays.
- Repeat with different pitches being altered.

166. Snapping High/Clapping Low

Concepts: High/low, pitch range recognition

- Students stand in their self-spaces.
- Students walk a steady beat in a tempo indicated by the teacher.

Meaningful Movement: A Music Teacher's Guide to Dalcroze Eurhythmics

- Teacher plays two different pitches on the piano or barred instrument as quarter notes (the farther apart the pitches, the easier it will be), followed by six beats of rest, then repeat those same two pitches and the students snap on the higher of the two pitches. Students are continually walking the beat.

- Teacher repeats this procedure several times using different pitches.
- Teacher repeats this procedure but asks the students to clap on the lower pitch.
- Teacher repeats this procedure with the students snapping (or clicking their tongue) on the higher pitch and clapping on the lower pitch.

167. Solfège Dictation

Concepts: Three-note melodic patterns, decoding with solfège

- Students stand in their self-spaces.
- Teacher sings various three-note melodic patterns (ex. *so-la-mi*) on solfège names followed by a rest and the students echo (Curwen hand signs can be added).

- Teacher discusses where the various solfège pitches are in terms of spatial relationships and asks students to find those solfège spaces on the floor using the spot where they are standing as the first pitch.
- Teacher plays three pitches followed by a rest on piano/barred instrument.
- Students echo the pattern by singing in solfège and move to the appropriate spaces.

Beginning Phase

168. Tonal Distraction (video clip)

Concept: Pitch memory

- Students sit on the floor.
- Teacher plays middle C on the piano and the students respond by singing *do, do, do,* (rest).
- Teacher plays a chord that contains "C" at the top and the students respond by singing *do, do, do,* (rest).

- Teacher plays a chord that contains "C" in the middle and the students respond by singing *do, do, do*, (rest).
- Teacher plays random chords that do not contain "C" and the students respond by singing *do, do, do*, (rest).

169. Gravity Scale

Concepts: Tonic scale degree, ascending/descending major scale

- Students sit in their chairs.
- As the teacher plays an ascending C major scale on the piano or barred instrument, the students slowly rise from their seats.
- As the teacher plays a descending C major scale, the students, slowly move down to their seats and are sitting when the teacher plays middle C.
- Teacher plays a partial scale (*do* to *so*) and students rise part way, lowering as the teacher plays.
- Teacher may vary the tempo and/or include *fermatas* especially on the last *re* to make sure students know where *do* is.
- Repeat this with the students singing the solfège instead of the teaching playing the C major scale.

170. Melodic Hopscotch

Concept: Same/different

- Students stand in their self-spaces.
- Teacher plays five pitches on the piano or a barred instrument.

- Teacher plays five pitches a second time with one different pitch. The students hop on one foot for the identical pitches and jump on two feet for the different pitch.

- Repeat with various pitches being altered.
- Repeat with more than one pitch being altered.

171. Snapping High/Clapping Low

Concepts: High/low, pitch range recognition

- Students stand in their self-spaces.
- Students walk a steady beat in a tempo indicated by the teacher.

- Teacher plays four different pitches as quarter notes followed by four beats of rest, then repeats the same pitch sequence and the students snap on the highest of the four pitches. Students are continually walking the beat.

- Teacher repeats this procedure several times using different pitch sequences.
- Repeat process but ask the students to clap on the lowest pitch.

172. Fly Back Home

Concepts: Finding the tonic in a song, inner hearing, quick reaction

- Students stand on their pre-assigned low *do* spots in their self-spaces.
- Teacher sings the song, "The Birdies Fly Away." Students act out the song based on the lyrics, leaving their nests (*do*) and returning on the word "home."

The Birdies Fly Away

Traditional

- Students sing the song and repeat the movement.
- Teacher plays the song on the piano. Children move but use inner hearing to perceive the lyrics.
- Teacher improvises a middle section to keep the students "flying around the room before returning to the nest" (quick reaction).

> **TEACHER CAN PUT STICKERS ON THE FLOOR TO INDICATE PRE-ASSIGNED *DO* SPOTS.** — *teacher tip*

173. Major Scale Quick Reaction

Concepts: Major scale, solfège, quarter note, eighth note, quick reaction

- Students stand in a circle facing in a counter-clockwise direction.
- Students sing a major scale in solfège and walk forward during the ascending scale and backwards during the descending scale.
- Students repeat the activity, but when the teacher plays the hand drum, the next pitch is sung as two eighth notes.

174. Dichords (video clip)

Concepts: Whole and half steps, dichords

- Students stand on their pre-assigned *do* spots in their self-spaces.
- Teacher plays or sings the following sequences and students echo step and sing.

- Repeat and the students show two fingers in open scissor position.
- Introduce *mi-fa*: students take smaller steps and show a two-finger closed scissor position.
- Students stand on *do* and step and sing the dichords: *do-re, re-mi, mi-fa*.
- Students step and sing descending dichords: *fa-mi, mi-re, re-do*.
- Students repeat this process with the second tetrachord. Students stand on a spot they have chosen for *so*: *so-la, la-ti, ti-do'*.
- Students repeat this process descending back to *so* (*do'-ti, ti-la, la-so*).
- Students step and sing the *do* to *do'* scale ascending in dichords; then descending in dichords. Stop on high *do'* to breathe before the descent.

- Students step backwards in the descent and end on their personal *do* spots.

Meaningful Movement: A Music Teacher's Guide to Dalcroze Eurhythmics

175. Tone Row Manipulation

Concepts: Inner hearing development, literacy

- Students stand in a line(s) facing the board.
- Teacher writes a five-measure diatonic row on the board.

- Students step and sing the pitches, filling in the intervals with steps in $\frac{4}{4}$ meter and with diatonic pitches.
- Students maintain a steady macro-beat and fill in the intervals within the macro-beat.

- Students step and sing the tone row in retrograde.
- Divide the students in half - one group sings and steps the original row, and one group steps and sings the row in retrograde. Repeat and switch roles.
- Students step all of the pitches, but sing only every other measure.

176. Solfège Dictation

Concepts: Decoding with solfège, melodic patterns

- Students stand on their pre-assigned *do* spots in their self-spaces.
- Teacher sings various three-note melodic patterns and the students echo-sing.
- Teacher discusses where the various solfège pitches are in relation to the scale and asks students to find those solfège spaces on the floor.
- Teacher plays three pitches on the piano or a barred instrument. (ex. *so-mi-do*)
- Students echo-sing the pattern in solfège and echo-step to the appropriate spaces in front or behind them.
- Repeat using four-note melodic patterns.

 **CURWEN HAND SIGNS CAN ALWAYS BE ADDED TO SOLFÈGE ACTIVITIES.**

Intermediate Phase

177. Invitation to "*Do*"

Concept: Tonic scale degree

- Students sit on the floor.
- Teacher plays low *so, la, ti* in the key of C on the piano and students sing *do* in the key of C.
- Repeat this pattern in different keys (movable *do*).

178. Tonal Distraction

Concept: Pitch memory

- Students sit on the floor.
- Teacher plays middle C on the piano and the students sing *do, do, do,* (rest).
- Teacher plays chords that contain "C" at the top, in the middle, and in the bottom of the chord, and the students respond by singing *do, do, do,* (rest).
- Teacher plays random chords that do not contain "C" and then the students sing *do, do, do,* (rest).
- Teacher plays a C major chord in various inversions; the students respond by singing *mi, re, do,* (rest).
- Teacher plays random major chords that do not contain C and students respond with *mi, re, do,* (rest).
- Teacher plays random minor chords and students respond with *mi, re, do,* (rest).

179. Gravity Scale

Concepts: Tonic scale degree, ascending/descending major scale

- Students sit in their chairs.
- As the teacher plays an ascending C major scale on the piano or a barred instrument, the students slowly rise from their seats.
- As the teacher plays a descending C major scale, the students slowly move down to their seats and are sitting when the teacher plays middle C.
- Teacher may vary tempo and/or include fermatas especially at the last *re* to make sure students know where *do* is.
- Teacher plays an ascending four-note C major broken chord; students respond to the ascending chord pitches by gradually moving to a standing position over four beats
- Teacher plays a descending four-note C major broken chord; students respond to the descending chord pitches by moving to a sitting position over four beats.
- Teacher plays a four-note C major broken chord out of order, (ex. C, G, E, high C). Students respond to each pitch with the appropriate distance between sitting and standing.

180. "*Do*" is Home

Concepts: Tonic scale degree, major scale

- Students stand on their pre-assigned *do* spots in their self-spaces.
- Students sing an ascending C major scale while walking the beat.
- When the teacher plays the hand drum, the students continue walking, but start singing the ascending scale from *do*.
- Students sing a descending C major scale while walking the beat. Upon hearing the hand drum, the students continue walking, but start singing the descending scale from high *do*.

181. Find your "*Do*"

Concept: Tonic scale degree

- Students stand on their pre-assigned *do* spots in their self-spaces.
- Teacher improvises a melodic line with traditional harmonies and students leave their *do* and walk around the space.
- When the teacher begins to play a passage moving towards a full cadence, slowing down the tempo, the students return to their *do*, arriving at the same time as the phrase ends with *do* and a I chord.

182. Scales with *hip* and *hop*

Concepts: Major and minor scales; modes; quick reaction; quarter, eighth, and half notes

- Students stand on their pre-assigned *do* spots in their self-spaces.
- Students walk to the beat and sing a *do* to *do* scale in a loop, not repeating the low *do* or the high *do* pitches.
- Teacher calls *hip* and the students maintain the same walking speed, but sing the scale twice as fast.
- Teacher calls *hop* and the students return to singing the same tempo as they are walking.
- Teacher calls *hop* and the students maintain the same walking tempo but sing the scale twice as slow.
- Students sing a *re* to *re* (dorian) mode.
- Teacher repeats the *hip* and *hop* with the dorian mode.
- Students sing a *la* to *la* (aeolean) mode.
- Teacher repeats the *hip* and *hop* with the aeolean mode.

183. Major Scale - Half/Whole Steps

Concepts: Major scale, half steps, whole steps, quick reaction

- Students stand in a circle facing counter-clockwise.

- Students sing a major scale in solfège and walk forward during the ascending scale and backwards during the descending scale. Students take smaller steps between the half steps (*mi-fa, ti-do*).

184. Major Scale - Inner Hearing

Concepts: Major scale, inner hearing, quick reaction

- Students are standing in a circle facing counter-clockwise.
- Students sing a major scale in solfège and walk forward during the ascending scale and backwards during the descending scale.
- Students repeat but when the teacher plays the hand drum, the next pitch(es) is/are sung internally until the hand drum plays again.

185. Major Scale in Solfège/Numbers/Letter Names

Concepts: Major scale, decoding with solfège

- Students stand on their pre-assigned *do* spots in their self-spaces.
- Students walk to the beat and sing a *do* to *do* scale in a loop, not repeating the low *do* or high *do* pitches.
- Students sing a C major scale using numbers (1-8) and walk the beat.
- Students sing a C major scale using letter names (C, D, E...) and walk the beat.
- Students begin by singing a C major scale using solfège and walk the beat but when the teacher plays the hand drum, the students change to numbers. When the teacher plays the hand drum again, the students change to letter names.

186. Major Scale in Meters/Rhythmic Patterns (video clip)

Concepts: Major scale, durations, rhythmic patterns, simple and compound meters

- Students stand on their pre-assigned *do* spots in their self-spaces.
- Students sing a C major scale, ascending and descending, to the following rhythmic patterns in the given meters. Students will clap these patterns while singing them with solfège, numbers, or letter names.

Meaningful Movement: A Music Teacher's Guide to Dalcroze Eurhythmics

187. Additive Major Scale (video clip)

Concept: Major scale

- Students stand in their self-spaces.
- Teacher sings the additive scale while the students conduct a four pattern.

- Teacher asks students to identify the pattern of the scale.
- Students sing the additive scale while conducting.
- Students sing the additive scale, conduct, and walk the beat.

188. Trichords (video clip)

Concepts: Whole and half steps, trichords

- Students stand on their pre-assigned *do* spots in their self-spaces.
- Teacher plays or sings the following sequences and students echo step and sing.

- Teacher reinforces *mi-fa* with the smaller step.
- Students stand on *do* and step/sing the trichords: *do-re-mi, re-mi-fa, mi-fa-so*.
- Students step and sing *so-fa-mi, fa-mi-re, mi-re-do*.
- Students step and sing the trichords of the second tetrachord. Students stand on *so*: *so-la-ti, la-ti-do', ti-do'-re'-do'*.
- Students step and sing the descending trichords down to *so* (*do'-ti-la, ti-la-so, la-so-fa, so*).

- Students step and sing the *do* to *do* ascending scale in trichords; then the *do* to *do* descending scale in trichords. Then students put them together and step and sing the ascending and descending scale, stopping to breathe on high *do* after the first half of the phrase. Students step backwards on the descending trichords and should end on their personal *do* spaces.

189. Trill Ornamentation

Concepts: Steps, trills, dichords

- Students stand in their self-spaces.
- Students sing a trill in eighth notes and walk the quarter beat, and then add conducting.

- Students repeat the descending trill pattern within the scale.

190. Snapping High/Clapping Low (video clip)

Concepts: High/low, pitch range recognition

- Students stand in their self-spaces.
- Students walk a steady beat in a tempo indicated by the teacher.
- Teacher plays four different pitches as quarter notes followed by four beats of rest, then repeats the same four pitches, and the students snap on the highest of the four pitches. Students are continually walking the beat.

- Teacher repeats this procedure several times with different pitches.
- Teacher repeats this procedure but the students clap on the lowest pitch.
- Teacher repeats this procedure several times with different pitches.
- Teacher repeats this procedure and the students snap on the highest pitch and clap on the lowest pitch.
- Teacher repeats this procedure several times with different pitches.

191. Fragmented Solfège

Concepts: Decoding with solfège, inner hearing, focus

- Students stand in their self-spaces.
- Students sing a familiar song with the lyrics while walking the beat.
- Students sing only on the first beat of each measure with the lyrics while walking the beat.
- Students are divided into two groups. Group "A" sings measure one, group "B" sings measure two, and they alternate measures for the rest of the song while walking the beat.
- Students switch to solfège, and sing only on beats one and two.
- Students are divided into two groups, and the groups sing alternate measures in solfège.
- All students sing the entire song in solfège.

192. Tone Row Manipulation

Concepts: Inner hearing, literacy, continuous canon, subdivision

- Students stand in a line(s) facing the board.
- Teacher writes a nine-measure diatonic row on the board.

- Students step and sing the pitches, filling in the intervals with steps in $\frac{4}{4}$ meter and with diatonic pitches.

- Students maintain a steady macro-beat and fill in the intervals within the macro-beat.
- Students step and sing the row in retrograde.
- Divide the students in half - one group sings and steps the original row, and one group steps and sings the row in retrograde.
- Switch roles.
- Divide the students in half and sing and step in canon two beats apart.
- Students sing the row in retrograde in canon.
- Students are assigned one of four starting points in the canon: forward, forward in canon, retrograde, retrograde in canon and sing the row.
- Students step all the pitches, but only sing every other measure (odd-numbered measures), using inner hearing for the silent measures.
- Repeat the previous step with even-numbered measures.
- Divide the students in half and have one group sing the row twice as fast (*hip*) and the other group sing the row at the original tempo. The group singing the row twice as fast needs to sing it two times.
- *Hip* in retrograde: Divide the students in half and have one group sing the row twice as fast (*hip*) in retrograde and the other group sing the row at the original tempo in retrograde. The group singing the row twice as fast needs to sing it two times.
- Teacher (or student) chooses one pitch not to sing out loud; ex. remain silent on all *so* pitches; omit more pitches until the group sings only one pitch.

193. "The Ghost of John"

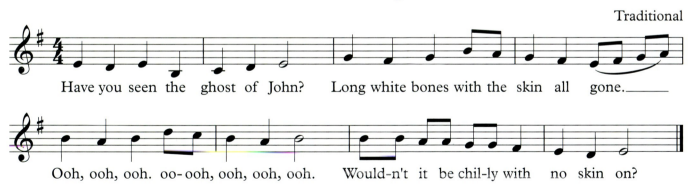

Concepts: Vocal improvisation in aeolean mode, minor scale, continuous canon

- Students stand on their pre-assigned *do* spots in their self-spaces.
- Students learn the song.
- Students sing a *la* to *la* minor scale on "loo" beginning on "E" (movable *do* system).

Meaningful Movement: A Music Teacher's Guide to Dalcroze Eurhythmics

- Teacher sings the first two measures on "loo". Students echo step following the melodic contour, and sing the phrase. Teacher continues singing two measure phrases and students echo step and sing them.
- Continue until the students can sing and step the entire melody.
- Students improvise a melody on the third phrase, "Ooh" section and step the melodic contour of their improvisations.
- Students sing and step the entire song with the third phrase improvised.
- Teacher shows the lyrics on the board and the students sing the song with the lyrics, walking the melodic contour, with the third phrase sung as written.
- Teacher divides the class in half and the students sing and step the whole piece in canon, with one half of the class four beats behind.

THIS SONG IS IN MOVABLE *DO* BUT CAN BE PERFORMED IN FIXED *DO* WITH STUDENTS STANDING ON THEIR *MI* SPOTS AND SINGING A *DO* TO *DO* SCALE WITH A LOWERED SEVENTH DEGREE AS PREPARATION.

194. Melodic/Rhythmic Dictation - Familiar Song

Concepts: Decoding with solfège, durations

- Students stand in their self-spaces.
- Teacher plays a familiar song on the piano or barred instrument.
- Students walk the beat and decode the solfège and rhythms of the song by singing the solfège and walking the melodic rhythm as the song is being played by the teacher.
- After multiple listenings, students sing the solfège and walk to the melodic rhythm of the piece without the teacher playing the song.

THIS CAN BE DONE IN EITHER FIXED *DO* OR MOVABLE *DO*.

195. Solfège Dictation

Concepts: Meter of five, melodic patterns, decoding with solfège

- Students stand in their self-spaces.
- Teacher sings various five note melodic patterns on "loo" and students echo with solfège.

- Teacher discusses where the various solfège pitches are in relation to the scale, and asks students to find those solfège spaces on the floor.
- Teacher plays five pitches on the piano or barred instrument. (ex. *do-mi-so-re-do*)
- Students echo the pattern in solfège and move to the appropriate spaces in front or behind them.

Advanced Phase

196. Snapping High/Clapping Low

Concepts: High/low, pitch range recognition

- Students stand in their self-spaces.
- Students walk a steady beat in a tempo indicated by the teacher.
- Teacher plays four different pitches as quarter notes followed by four beats of rest. Then the teacher repeats the sequence and the students snap on the highest of the four pitches.

- Students are continually walking the beat.
- Teacher repeats this procedure several times with different pitch sequences.
- Teacher repeats the process but asks the students to clap on the lowest pitch.
- Teacher repeats the process but asks the students to snap on the highest pitch and clap on the lowest pitch.
- Teacher inserts eighth notes into the phrase.
- Teacher increases the phrase length to eight beats.
- Teacher changes the meter to $\frac{3}{4}$ or $\frac{6}{8}$.

197. Major/Minor Scale Quick Reaction

Concepts: Major scale, minor scale, durations, half step/whole step, inner hearing, quick reaction

- Students stand in a circle facing counter-clockwise.
- Students sing a major scale ascending and descending repeating high *do* while they walk the beat, walking forward for ascending and backwards for descending.
- Students sing a major scale ascending and descending repeating high *do* while they walk the beat, walking forward for ascending and backwards for descending. They indicate the half steps by taking smaller steps.
- Students sing a major scale ascending and descending, repeating high *do* and walk the beat forward and backwards. When the teacher signals with the hand drum, the students sing the next solfège pitch as two eighth notes and step two eighth notes.

- Students repeat the activity with the teacher playing the hand drum at various places in the scale.
- Students sing a major scale ascending and descending repeating high *do* while they walk the beat forward and backwards. When the teacher signals with the hand drum, the students sing inside their heads but continue walking the beat, and when the teacher signals with the drum they sing out loud.
- Students repeat the activity with the teacher signaling with the hand drum at different places.
- Students repeat the activity using a minor scale, dorian, and aeolean modes.

198. Major/Minor Scale in Solfège/Numbers/Letter Names

Concepts: Major scale, minor scale, decoding with solfège

- Students stand in their self-spaces.
- Students sing a C major scale using solfège and walk the beat.
- Students sing a C major scale using numbers and walk the beat.
- Students sing a C major scale using letter names and walk the beat.
- Students begin by singing a C major scale using solfège and walk the beat but when the teacher plays the hand drum, the students change to numbers. When teacher plays the hand drum again, the students change to letter names.
- Repeat steps using a C minor scale.
- Repeat in d-dorian and a-aeolean modes.

199. Major/Minor Scale in Meters/Rhythmic Patterns with Syncopation

Concepts: Major scale, minor scale, syncopation, simple and compound meters

- Students stand on their pre-assigned *do* spots in their self-spaces.
- Students sing a C major scale using various rhythmic patterns and meters (use solfège, numbers, or letters) and clap three patterns.

- Students repeat the process using a C minor scale.
- Students repeat the process using modes.

200. Additive Major/Minor Scale

Concepts: Major scale, minor scale, continuous canon

- Students stand in their self-spaces.
- Teacher sings the additive scale while the students conduct a four pattern.

- Teacher asks students to identify the pattern.
- Students sing the additive scale while conducting.
- Students sing the additive scale, conduct, and walk the beat.
- Students divide into two groups and sing the additive scale in canon two beats apart.
- Students divide into four groups and sing the additive scale in canon four beats apart.
- Students divide into two groups and one group starts singing the ascending additive scale while the other group starts singing the descending additive scale.
- Students divide into two groups and one group starts singing the ascending additive scale while the other group sings the descending additive scale in canon, two beats later.
- Students repeat these steps using a minor scale.

201. Turn Ornamentation

Concepts: Steps, turns, trichords

- Students stand in their self-spaces.
- Students sing a turn (*do-re-do-ti,-do rest, re-mi-re-do-re rest, etc.*) while walking the beat.

Meaningful Movement: A Music Teacher's Guide to Dalcroze Eurhythmics

- Students repeat the previous step and add conducting a four pattern.
- Students repeat the descending scale with turns.

 **MAKE SURE THE PITCHES STAY DIATONIC.**

202. Fragmented Song/Solfège

Concepts: Decoding with solfège, focus

- Students stand in their self-spaces.
- Students sing a familiar song while walking the beat.
- Students only sing on the first and last beats of each measure maintaining a steady beat in the feet.
- Students only sing on the second and third beats of each measure while walking on the beat.
- Students are divided into two groups. One group sings on beats one and four and the other group sings on beats two and three while walking the beat.
- Students are divided into two groups that sing alternating measures while walking the beat.
- Students repeat the process by singing the song using solfège.
- Students repeat the process with an unfamiliar song they are sight-reading from the board.
- Students reverse the process by starting with solfège with a different unfamiliar song written on the board.

203. Sight-Reading in Canon - "Water Canon"

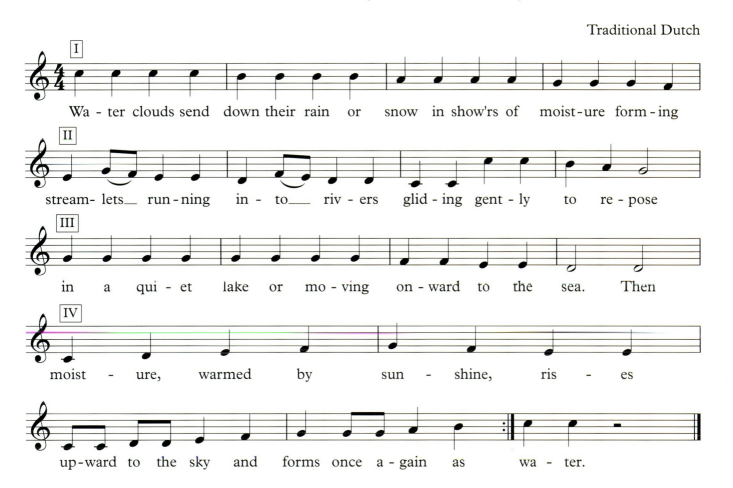

Water Canon (Vatenkanon)

Traditional Dutch

Concepts: Literacy, continuous canon

- Students stand in their self-spaces.
- Students sing the song using solfège on beats one and four while walking the beat.
- Students sing the song using solfège on beats two and three while walking the beat.
- Students are divided in half: one group sings the song using solfège on beats one and four and the other group sings the song using solfège on beats two and three while walking the beat.
- All students sing the entire song on solfège while walking the beat.
- Students sing the song with the lyrics in canon while walking the beat.
- Students are divided into four parts and sing the song in canon while walking the beat.

204. Tone Row Manipulation

Concepts: Literacy, continuous canon, inner hearing

- Students stand in a line(s) facing the board.

- Teacher writes a fifteen-measure diatonic row on the board.

- Students step and sing the pitches, filling in the intervals with steps in $\frac{4}{4}$ meter and with diatonic pitches.

- Students maintain a steady macro-beat and fill in the intervals within the macro-beat.
- Students step and sing the row in retrograde.
- Divide the students in half - one group sings and steps the original row, and one group steps and sings the row in retrograde.
- Switch roles.
- Divide the students in half and sing and step in canon two beats apart.
- Students sing the row in retrograde in canon.
- Students are assigned one of four starting points in the canon: forward, forward in canon, retrograde, retrograde in canon and sing the row.
- Students step all the pitches, but only sing every other measure (odd-numbered measures), using inner hearing for the silent measures.
- Repeat the previous step with even-numbered measures.
- Divide the students in half and have one group sing the row at twice as fast (*hip*) and the other group sing the row at the original tempo. The group singing the row twice as fast needs to sing it two times.
- *Hip* in retrograde: Divide the students in half and have one group sing the row twice as fast (*hip*) in retrograde and the other group sing the row at the original tempo in retrograde. The group singing the row twice as fast needs to sing it two times.
- Teacher (or student) chooses one pitch not to sing out loud; ex. remain silent on all *so* pitches; omit more pitches until the group sings only one pitch.

- Teacher asks the students to alter one designated pitch: i.e. all *fa* pitches become sharp to *fi*.
- Students work in groups to create a nine-measure tone row and then find ways to manipulate the row.
- Students present their tone rows.

205. Solfège Dictation

Concepts: Melodic patterns, literacy

- Students stand in their self-spaces.
- Teacher sings various six to ten-note melodic patterns and the students echo.

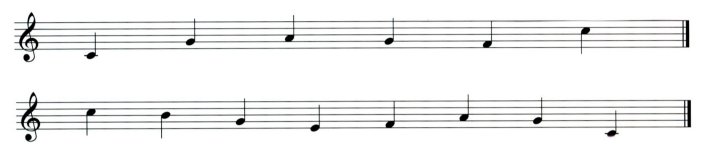

- Teacher discusses where the various solfège pitches are in relation to the scale and asks students to find those solfège spaces on the floor.
- Teacher plays six to ten pitches on the piano or barred instrument.
- Students echo the pattern in solfège and move to the appropriate spaces in front of or behind them.

206. Rhythmic/Melodic Dictation of an Unknown Piece of Music

Concepts: Rhythmic and melodic dictation, decoding with solfège, durations, music memory

- Students stand in their self-spaces.
- Teacher plays the melodic line of a short, unknown piece of music (eight-twelve measures).
- Teacher plays *do*, sets the tempo and plays the piece several times. Students begin by walking the beat while they try to figure out the rhythm.
- Students walk the melodic rhythm as they learn it (individual progress).
- After the students have the melodic rhythm, they should begin to listen for the melody and sing inaudibly the solfège as they learn it.
- After many listenings, the students should be able to walk the melodic rhythm and sing the melody in solfège.
- Teacher shows the music on the board to the students who then read it and sing it together. The students can then assess their own performances.

THE DIFFICULTY OF THE PIECE DEPENDS ON THE STUDENTS' DEVELOPMENTAL READINESS.

CHAPTER SIX

KEYBOARD IMPROVISATION

As children improvise movement, the teacher can support and encourage the improvisation from the keyboard. This chapter provides some tips for keyboard improvisation in the classroom. If you have not improvised for movement before, use these ideas to get started, and then experiment on your own. You can approach beginning improvisation two ways. First, you play and watch how the students move and you accompany their movements from the keyboard. You can also ask the students to move in a certain way, and then accompany their movement with music that fits what you see them doing.

Tools for Improvisation:

As the teacher, your essential purpose in improvisation is to lead the movement from the keyboard. How you do it is up to you. Here are some suggestions:

- Use the black keys to create a pentatonic improvisation.
- Use atonal harmonies that incorporate a series of open fifth intervals.
- Use atonal harmonies where one hand is on the black keys and the other hand is on the white keys.
- Incorporate modes, particularly aeolean, dorian, and mixolydian, to open up the ears of the children.
- Create chord progressions in a few keys: I – IV – V – I, or I - vi – IV – V – I.

The most common movements for children are:

- Walking
- Marching
- Running
- Gliding
- Skipping
- Jumping

Walking is often initiated in common time. The chart (right) indicates the tempi at which children are most comfortable walking and marching.

Walking Tempi in Steps Per Minute

Grade	Walking	Marching
Pre-K	139	139
K	140	139
1	149	140
2	148	139
3	141	138
4	137	129
5	135	126
6	133	124

Meaningful Movement: A Music Teacher's Guide to Dalcroze Eurhythmics

Try this! Place your left hand in a five-finger position where your fifth finger is on the tonic and your thumb is on the dominant. Place your right hand in the same five-five finger position one octave higher. In the left hand, play four steady beats on the tonic, getting gradually louder. This tells the children the tempo. Continue with a *legato* tonic/dominant pattern in your left hand. Your right hand can create a simple melody that has an antecedent and consequent phrase. Here is a short example.

Marching music is similar to walking, and can be played in meters of two or four. It is important to detach the sound in the left hand. This encourages the children to lift their feet higher off the floor. To enhance the right hand, try playing the following score in thirds.

Running music is light and slightly detached. In order to establish the tempo, watch the children running in the room and take their tempo. Similar to walking, you can use a tonic/dominant repeated pattern in your left hand, i.e. C & G. Think about extending your left-hand options to leading tone and dominant, i.e. low B & G. Children will be attending to your left hand so keep the tempo steady. What you play in the right hand can be simple and sparse.

Gliding music is most often in a meter of three. It involves sustained chords on beat one, preceded by an anacrusis that motivates the person to lift a foot before gliding. Place your hands close together and experiment with non-tonal harmonies—perhaps random seventh chords.

Skipping music is in compound duple meter. The left hand plays dotted quarter notes on beats one and four and the right hand plays combinations of dotted quarter notes, quarter/eighth note combinations, and running eighth notes. The student pushes off, leaving the ground, on the macrobeats (dotted quarter notes) in the left hand. The right hand should sound playful and light. Many pre-K and kindergarten children will be galloping. You can use the same music, but know that the leading foot will match the left hand.

Jumping music is in a fast duple meter and can be played atonally or tonally. The left hand plays a note low on the keyboard and the right hand plays a three-note splash mid-way up the keyboard. The lower note coincides with the students' knee bend. The splash matches the jump. Varying the dynamics and the distance between the lower note and the splash will encourage the students to jump higher.

SEQUENCING THE DALCROZE APPROACH

PHASE	CONCEPTS	FOCUS	RHYTHM	MELODY	HARMONY	EXPRESSION
Introductory	Steady Beat High/Low Tonic/Dominant Expressive Movement	#4 Start/Stop	#38 Walking Various Rhythmic Patterns	#42 Walking Bass/ Clapping Treble (isolated)	#41 I, V7	#43 "Kangaroos" Saint-Saëns *Legato, staccato* High/low
Beginning	Steady beat Macro-beat/Micro-beat High/Low Tonic/Dominant/ Subdominant Expressive Movement	#11 Passing the Beat	#46 Macro-beat/ Micro-beat	#68 Walking Bass/ Clapping Treble (simultaneously)	#66 I, IV, V7	#44 "Fossils" Saint-Saëns Rhythmic patterns Style
Intermediate	Durations Subdivisions Tonic/Dominant/ Subdominant/ Submediant	#21 Apple/ Pear Opposites	#74 Hip and Hop/ Subdivision	#186 Major Scale in Meters/Rhythmic Patterns	#96 I, IV, V7, vi	#130 "Luminosa" Libera Diamond Shadowing in Quartets
Advanced	Syncopation Minor tonality - Tonic/Dominant/ Subdominant/ Submediant Expressive Movement	#26 Alphabet/ Number	#103 Syncopation "Ivan Sings" Khatchaturian	#199 Major/Minor Scale in Meters/ Rhythmic Patterns with Syncopation	#113 Harmonic Dictation with i, iv, V7, VI	#137 "Oblivion" Piazzolla Syncopation, Flow, Dynamics

Glossary

Anacrusis - preparation to/of the crusis, an increase of energy in the body including the breath

Anapest phrase - a short/short/long phrase, i.e. quarter/quarter/half

Body percussion - using the body to create sounds to represent the elements of music

Circular clapping - clapping the hands, starting from bottom to top making a circle. Shows time, space, and energy; increases musicality and accuracy of the beat

Compound meter - a meter with subdivisions of three

Continuous canon - a follow (echo) starting with a prescribed number of beats or measures behind the leader (first voice)

Crusis - the point of arrival

Curwen hand signs - hand signs to represent solfège syllables developed by John Curwen in England in the mid-19th century

Dactylic phrase - a long/short/short phrase, i.e. half/quarter/quarter

Dichords - two adjacent melodic steps, i.e. *do-re*, *re-mi*, *mi-fa*, etc.

Durations - note values

Eurhythmics - "good flow" expressing music through movement in an artistic and accurate manner

Fixed *do* - C is *do* regardless of the key

Hip and hop - cues, i.e. "hip" is twice as fast, "hop" is twice as slow

Inner hearing - internalization of pitch, melody, and/or rhythm

Interrupted canon - a musical event is echoed

Locomotor - movement through space from one place to another place

Macro-beat - the beat that feels to be the longest, i.e. in a fast tempo in $\frac{3}{4}$ meter - dotted half notes are the macro-beats

Metacrusis - the follow through, continuation of the rhythmic movement following the crusis

Micro-beat - the beat that feels to be the shortest, i.e. in a fast tempo in 3/4 meter - quarter notes are the micro-beats

Movable *do* - *Do* is established as the tonic of the key

Non-locomotor - body movement without traveling from one place to another

Nuance - a subtle, expressive variation in music

Ostinato - a repeated pattern

Plastique animée - the artistic and creative embodiment of the music through individual or group movement

Quick reaction - a movement change in response to a musical or verbal cue

Retrograde - backwards, from end to beginning

Rhythmic solfège - using solfège with locomotor or non-locomotor movement

Self-space - students are standing anywhere in a classroom (within perimeters set by teacher) and are facing any direction, ideally, not in close proximity to another student

Simple meter - a meter with subdivisions of two

Split second imitation - imitation in real time happening immediately when the student perceives the motion or sound

Tetrachord - four adjacent melodic steps involving major and minor seconds

Time, space, and energy - interrelated elements in music where time is a rhythmic element, space is the physical relationship of the movement, and energy is the force/effort of the movement

Trichords - three adjacent melodic steps, i.e. *do-re-mi*, *re-mi-fa*, *mi-fa-so*, etc.

Music Recordings

Lesson #	Title	Composer	Suggested Recording
45	A Mover La Colita	Lacopetti/Sarmiento	La Sonora Dinamita
155	Adagio for Strings	Barber, Samuel	Zurich Baroque Strings
48	Air on the G String	Bach, J.S.	Jean-François Paillard
91	All You Need is Love	McCartney, Paul	Yellow Submarine Soundtrack
85	America	Smith, Samuel Francis	
102	Après un Rêve	Fauré, Gabriel	Kiri Te Kanawa
141	Aquarium	Saint-Saëns, Camille	Carnival of the Animals
64, 95	Are You Sleeping	Folk Song	
125, 149	Baba Yetu	Tin, Christopher	Calling All Dawns
106	Blue Rondo à la Turk	Brubeck, Dave	Time Out
81	Bottom	Zap Mama	Adventures in Afropea
131	Brandenburg Concerto #6, 1st Mvt.	Bach, J.S.	Tafelmuzik
74	Central Time	LaFarge, Pokey	Pokey LaFarge
46, 150	Cider House Rules Main Theme	Portman, Rachel	Cider House Rules Soundtrack
108	Clapping Music	Reich, Steve	Early Works
77	Clowns	Kabalevsky, Dmitri	Hiroshi Arimori
93	Connla's Well	Adiemus	The Celts
132	Devil's Beauties	Dompierre, François	Infernal Violins
54	Double Trouble	Williams, John	Harry Potter and the Prisoner of Azkaban
135	Dream is Collapsing	Zimmer, Hans	Inception
142	Elephants	Saint-Saëns, Camille	Carnival of the Animals
72	Ever, Ever After	Menken/Schwartz	Enchanted Soundtrack
56	Fight Song	Platten, Rachel	Wildfire
151	Flying Theme	Williams, John	E.T. Soundtrack
144	Fossils	Saint-Saëns, Camille	Carnival of the Animals
121, 145	Gabriel's Oboe	Morricone, Ennio	The Mission Soundtrack
87	Hello	Adele	25
65	Hey, Betty Martin	Folk Song	
133	Hymn Do Trójcy Świętej	Tin, Christopher	Calling All Dawns
129	Il Deserto	Morricone, Ennio	The Good, the Bad, and the Ugly
92	In Freezing Winter Night	Britten, Benjamin	A Ceremony of Carols
59	In the Hall of the Mountain King	Grieg, Edvard	London Philharmonic Orchestra
57, 82, 103	Ivan Sings	Khachaturian, Aram	
152	Jurassic Park Theme	Williams, John	Jurassic Park
143	Kangaroos	Saint-Saëns, Camille	Carnival of the Animals
138	Knee I	Glass, Philip	Einstein on the Beach
157	Lacrymosa	Mozart, W.A.	Requiem
136	Let it Go	Lopez, Robert	Frozen Soundtrack
62	Li'l Liza Jane	Folk Song	
41	London Bridge	Folk Song	

Lesson #	Title	Composer	Suggested Recording
48	Love Song	Bareilles, Sara	Little Voice
130	Luminosa	Libera	Luminosa
146	Lumos!	Williams, John	Harry Potter and the Prisoner of Azkaban
49	Menuet	Handel, G. F.	Water Music
105	Mikrokosmos #33	Bartok, Bela	Jenö Jandó
156	Mille Echi	Morricone, Ennio	La Piovra
98	Minuet BWV 115	Bach, J.S.	Anna Magdelena Bach Book
139	Miserere	Chant	
88	Mission Impossible Theme	Elfman, Danny	Mission Impossible Soundtrack
128	Moonlight Sonata	Beethoven, L. von	Vladimir Ashkenazy
159	Nimrod	Elgar, Edward	Enigma Variations
163	Nocturne	Morricone, Ennio	The Lady Caliph
147	O Fortuna	Orff, Carl	Carmina Burana
137, 160	Oblivion	Piazzolla, Astor	Operassion
161	Pavanne	Fauré, Gabriel	Academy of St. Martin in the Fields
109	Psalm 23	Rutter, John	Requiem
124	Recordare	Libera	Eternal: The Best of Libera
63	Rocky Mountain	Folk Song	
153	Romeo and Juliet	Prokofiev, Serge	Cleveland Orchestra
53	Row, Row, Row Your Boat	Folk Song	Traditional
67	Sad, Sad Day	Waters, Muddy	King Bee
162	Sand	Lanier, Nathan	Sand
110	Scherzo on Tenth Avenue	Kraehenbuehl, David	
127	Song for Viola	Adams, Peter Bradley	Leavetaking
49	Stars and Stripes for Ever	Sousa, John Phillip	President's Own Marine Band
154	Superman Theme	Williams, John	Superman Soundtrack
148	Swan	Saint-Saëns, Camille	Carnival of the Animals
84	Symphony #7, 2nd Mvt.	Beethoven, L. von	Chicago Symphony Orchestra
89	Take Five	Brubeck, Dave	Time Out
158	Tango Sensations: Fear	Piazzolla, Astor	Essential Tangos
49	Tell My Ma	Rankin Family	Fare Thee Well Love
172	The Birdies Fly Away	Folk Song	
193	The Ghost of John	Folk Song	
79, 111	The Happy Farmer	Schumann, Robert	
47	Trumpet Concerto in D (Allegro)	Torelli, Giuseppe	
90	Unsquare Dance	Brubeck, Dave	Dave Brubeck's Greatest Hits
164	Unstoppable	Posthumus, E. S.	
134	Voca Me	Libera	Eternal: The Best of Libera
203	Water Canon	Forsser, Stefan	

Music Literature Genre Categories

Classical
"Adagio for Strings" Barber
"Air on the G String" Bach
"Après un Rêve" Fauré
"Aquarium" *Carnival of the Animals* Saint-Saëns
"Brandenburg Concerto #6" 1st Mvt. Bach
"Clapping Music" Reich
"Clowns" Kabelevsky
"Devil's Beauties" Dompierre
"Elephants" *Carnival of the Animals* Saint-Saëns
"Fossils" *Carnival of the Animals* Saint-Saëns
"In Freezing Winter Night" *A Ceremony of Carols* Britten
"In the Hall of the Mountain King" Grieg
"Ivan Sings" Khachaturian
"Kangaroos" *Carnival of the Animals* Saint-Saëns
"Knee I" from *Einstein on the Beach* Glass
"Lacrymosa" *Requiem* Mozart
"Menuet" *Water Music* Handel
"Mikrokosmos" #33 Bartok
"Minuet" BWV 115 Anna Magdelena Bach
"Miserere" Chant
"Moonlight Sonata" Beethoven
"Nimrod" *Enigma Variations* Elgar
"O Fortuna" *Carmina Burana* Orff
"Oblivion" Piazzolla
"Pavanne" Fauré
"Psalm 23" Rutter
"Romeo and Juliet" Prokofiev
"Scherzo on Tenth Avenue" Kraehenbuehl
Symphony #7, 2nd Mvt. Beethoven
"Swan" *Carnival of the Animals* Saint-Saëns
"Tango Sensations: Fear" Piazzolla
"The Happy Farmer" Schumann
"Trumpet Concerto in D," (Allegro) Torelli

Pop
"All You Need is Love" McCartney
"Fight Song" Platten
"Hello" Adele
"Love Song" Bareilles

Multicultural
"A Mover La Colita" Lacopetti/Sarmiento
"Baba Yetu" Tin
"Bottom" Zap Mama
"Hymn Do Trójcy Świętej (Hymn to the Holy Trinity)" Tin
"Tell My Ma" The Rankin Family
"Water Canon" (Dutch Canon)

Jazz/Blues
"Blue Rondo à la Turk" Brubeck
"Central Time" Pokey LaFarge
"Sad, Sad Day" Muddy Waters
"Take Five" Brubeck
"Unsquare Dance" Brubeck

Folk/Patriotic Songs
"Are You Sleeping?"
"America" Key
"Hey, Betty Martin"
"Li'l Liza Jane"
"London Bridge"
"Rocky Mountain"
"Row, Row, Row Your Boat"
"Stars and Stripes Forever" Sousa
"The Birdies Fly Away"
"The Ghost of John"

Film Music
"Cider House Rules Main Theme" Portman
"Connla's Well" *The Celts* Adiemus
"Double Trouble" *Harry Potter: Prisoner of Azkaban* Williams
"Dream is Collapsing" *Inception* Zimmer
"Ever, Ever After" *Enchanted* Menken/Schwartz
"Flying Theme" *E.T.* Williams
"Gabriel's Oboe" *The Mission* Morricone
"Il deserto" *The Good, the Bad, and the Ugly* Morricone
"Jurassic Park Theme" Williams
"Let it Go" *Frozen* Lopez
"Lumos!" *Harry Potter: Prisoner of Azkaban* Williams
"Mille echi" *La Piovra* Morricone
"Mission Impossible Theme" Elfman
"Nocturne" *The Lady Caliph* Morricone
"SupermanTheme" Williams

Contemporary
"Luminosa" Libera
"Recordare" Libera
"Sand" Lanier
"Song for Viola" Adams
"Unstoppable" Posthumus
"Voca Me" Libera

Notes

Notes